NO NONSENSE
FLY FISHING GUIDEBOOKS

www.nononsenseguides.com

11-03

The No Nonsense Creed

The best way to go fly fishing is to find out a little something about a water, and then just go. Trying, figuring, wrong turns, surprises, self-reliance and discovering something new, even in familiar waters, are what make the memories.

The next best way is to learn enough from a local to save you from going too far wrong. You'll still find the water on your own, and it still feels as if you were the first.

This is the idea for our unique No Nonsense fly fishing series. Our books reveal little hush-hush information, yet they give all you need to find what will become your own secret places.

Painstakingly pared down, our writing is elegantly simple. Each title offers a local fly fishing expert's candid tour of favorite fly fishing waters. Nothing is over-sold or out of proportion. Everything is authentic, especially the discoveries and experiences you get after using our books.

No Nonsense Fly Fishing Guidebooks give you a quick, clear, understanding of the essential information needed to fly fish a region's most outstanding waters. The authors are highly experienced and qualified local fly fishers. Maps are tidy versions of the author's sketches.

About These Books

The publisher is located in the tiny Western town of Sisters, Oregon, just a few miles from the Metolius River. A couple of fly fishers create No Nonsense books, including Pete Chadwell who does all the layout, illustrations and maps. This work is a testament to his accuracy and desire to get out and fly fish new waters.

All who produce these books believe in providing top quality products at reasonable prices. We also believe all information should be confirmed whenever possible. We never hesitate to go out, fly rod in hand, to verify the facts and figures that appear in the pages of our books. The staff is committed to this grueling research. It's dirty work, but we're glad to do it for you.

For more on No Nonsense Fly Fishing Guidebooks, our authors, and some neat fly fishing stuff, visit www.nononsenseguides.com.

Conservation

No Nonsense Fly Fishing Guidebooks believes that, in addition to local information and gear, fly fishers need clean water and healthy fish. We encourage preservation, improvement, conservation, enjoyment and understanding of our waters and their inhabitants. While fly fishing, take care of the place, practice catch & release.

When you aren't fly fishing, a good way to help all things wild and aquatic is to support organizations dedicated to these ideas. No Nonsense Fly Fishing Guidebooks does and is a member, sponsor of and donor to organizations that preserve what we cherish.

Fly Fishing Lee's Ferry Arizona

The Complete Guide to Fishing and Boating the Colorado River Below Glen Canyon Dam

Dave Foster

Illustrated by Pete Chadwell

Fly Fishing Lee's Ferry, Arizona
The Complete Guide to Fishing and Boating The Colorado River
Below Glen Canyon Dam
ISBN #1-892469-07-3

© 2002 No Nonsense Fly Fishing Guidebooks
Published By
No Nonsense Fly Fishing Guidebooks • Sisters, Oregon 97759
www.nononsenseguides.com

Author: Dave Foster
Editors: David Banks, Helen Condon
Maps, Illustrations & Production: Pete Chadwell
Fold-Out Map: Charley Engle, Pete Chadwell
Fold-Out Photos: Dave Foster, Gary Ladd, Barbara Foster
Cover Photo: Dave Foster
Back Cover Photos: Gary Ladd, Barbara Foster
Printed By:

Hignell Book Printing
488 Burnell Street
Winnipeg, Manitoba
Canada R3G 2B4

Disclaimer: While this guide will greatly help readers to fly fish, it is not a substitute for caution, good judgment and the services of a qualified fly fishing guide or outfitter.

This book is dedicated to Larry Echave

Is it Lee's, Lees or Lee?

Over the years, a debate has raged over the spelling of Lee's Ferry. Is it Lee's Ferry, Lees Ferry or Lee Ferry? Various institutions have used all three.

The United States Board on Geographical Names has a policy (from the 1890's) that omits apostrophes before or after the possessive "s". They reason the apostrophe could get "lost" in maps or become confused with navigation symbols on charts. The 1922 Colorado River Compact (see Glen Canyon Dam section) coined the word Lee Ferry to describe the point of division between the upper and lower basin states.

Lee's Ferry is seemingly grammatically correct. The apostrophe, a symbol introduced during the 16th and 17th centuries, indicates the omission of one or more letters. For example, "Lee, his ferry" gets changed to "Lee's Ferry". This is the version we have chosen to use.

Photo by Dave Foster.

Table of Contents

Acknowledgements

The author and publisher acknowledge the many fine works and personal accounts that contributed to this book. A complete list of referenced works and other reading is listed in the appendix.

Foreword

Our No Nonsense Fly Fishing Guidebooks provide essential information on where to fly fish. We do this with detailed maps and without a lot of wasted motion or "falderal" as our original author, Harry Teel, put it.

Fly Fishing Lee's Ferry, by Dave Foster, provides more than enough information on where to fly fish. More words than in our typical guides, however, are necessary to understand and appreciate Lee's Ferry.

The magnitude and uniqueness of this remote destination screams for a more detailed overview, which could run several thick volumes. Understanding the dam flows alone could be a boxed set.

A hallmark of our titles, though, is well-organized, concise information. Dave Foster's vast understanding of his huge home waters is pared down to the essentials here.

True to our creed, we also include additional no nonsense "Where To" information in the Nearby Fly Fishing section at the back of this book.

David Banks

Sisters, Oregon
July 2002

Towering cliffs of Glen Canyon. Photo by Dave Foster.

Fly Fishing Lee's Ferry

Lee's Ferry is unique in that it can present the angler with a wide array of fishing situations. Few rivers can confront and possibly confound a fisherman with so many methods and variations in one stretch of water. In a single riffle you may change from dry fly fishing to shallow water nymphing and back to casting tiny dries in a matter of a couple of hours as conditions change. If you are inadequately or improperly equipped, you will find certain fishing situations frustrating and will not be able to take full advantage of what the river has to offer.

Rods

When selecting a rod for Lee's Ferry, look mainly for line control and versatility. It is not usually necessary to make long casts. For this reason, we suggest a five-weight at least nine feet long with a moderate to soft action. Rods of this length improve line control and facilitate hook setting on extended drifts. Softer action rods mend and feed slack more efficiently and also help protect the light tippets often used. Stiffer, fast action rods tend to mend poorly and are often the reason fish break off when using light tippets. A five-weight is ideal because it is heavy enough for most nymph fishing situations, but is still fun and effective when casting tiny dries in a back eddy.

Some anglers will want to carry a second rod for dry fly fishing. A four-weight of nine feet is perfect for Lee's Ferry. Lighter and shorter rods are fun to fool around with but are of very limited use here.

Reels

Although a great variety of high-end reels have come on the market in the past several years, Lee's Ferry is really no different than most trout fisheries when it comes to fly reel selection. The only requirements are that the reel have a rim control spool, adequate backing, and be reliable. More elaborate drag systems are nice, but not imperative. Fly reel selection for trout fishing is largely a matter of taste and style and a reel should be a pleasure to use.

Waders

The Colorado River in this stretch averages 48-50 degrees year round and chest waders are a necessity. Although most wading is in water less than thigh deep, chest waders are the norm because of safety considerations and versatility. This is not a good river for hip boots. By far the most popular waders are breathables. These are a delight to wear during hot weather and are warm enough for mid-winter use when coupled with adequate clothing underneath. Neoprene waders are fine for late fall, winter and early spring, but can be unbearable in the summer. Even during the summer months, most anglers find wet wading extremely uncomfortable for more than a few minutes. While some do it, wet wading is not recommended.

Much of the wading in this stretch of the Colorado is relatively mild. The river bottom is generally sand, small gravel, or cobbles up to eight to ten inches in diameter. With a couple of exceptions, the river is mercifully without "greased bowling ball" wading. Cleats are not necessary but wading shoes should have a good pair of felt soles and provide adequate support. A wading staff may help some anglers and, of course, you need a wading belt.

Flylines

Most Lee's Ferry fly fishing, especially dead drift presentations, requires floating lines. Whether weight forward or double taper is best is debatable as each has advantages. Double tapers generally mend, roll cast and handle more easily, as they carry more weight in the belly of the flyline. When casting longer leaders and heavy nymphing rigs, weight forward lines turn leaders over more easily. In either instance, use a flyline that is visible. In most fishing situations visible flylines do not spook fish and, for most fishermen, the advantage of seeing and understanding what the flyline is doing during the drift outweighs any perceived disadvantages. If you are convinced that a visible fly line is ruining your fishing, color the last fifteen feet with shoe polish or a permanent marker.

Leaders

Tapered monofilament leaders $7\frac{1}{2}$ to 9 feet are the standard at Lee's Ferry. Avoid hand tied leaders because all those knots just catch moss and can tangle easily. Avoid braided leaders that don't sink as quickly as mono. Bring tippet sizes 3x - 7x. For nymphing 5x - 6x is the norm. Many anglers are using fluorocarbon tippet when fishing is tough because it has the same light refractory characteristics as water and is nearly invisible. Given the clarity of the water at Lee's Ferry, it is certainly justifiable. A spool of 5x - 6x fluorocarbon is not a bad idea. Remember, it is slightly weaker than mono of the same diameter.

13

Split Shot

Getting the fly to the proper depth is the most important aspect of presentation on this river, period. Neither fly selection nor drag-free drift matters if the fly is not fine-tuned to the proper depth. A good selection of shot for the Ferry includes sizes AB, BB, #1, #4, #6 and #8. I suggest non-toxic shot because of environmental concerns and it tends to hold its position on the leader better. Some sort of "soft lead" weight can also be helpful. This gummy material, with lead or tin powder, is molded on the leader and is most useful when adding a very small amount of weight to a dropper below a dry fly. It is absolutely useless in cold weather.

Strike Indicators

A month does not go by that I do not have to defuse criticism and disgust at the use of indicators. Successful short line nymphing without an indicator is easy because one never fishes much more line than twice the length of the rod. It is impossible, however, to detect a strike on a thirty to eighty foot drag-free drift without a strike indicator. Even then, it still requires attention to minute changes in the drift of the indicator to see all the takes. This is because much of our fishing utilizes leaders of ten to twelve feet or more. It takes a long time for a strike to be transmitted through such a long leader and it is likely to be a very faint signal, at that. Also, because current speed in a river varies vertically as well as horizontally, the leader's path from indicator to fly is anything but a straight line. This further serves to slow the transmission of the take to the indicator and influences exactly what an indicator might do when a fish does take the fly. Depending on the configuration of the leader in relation to the indicator, the indicator may simply stop in the current, accelerate down current, move to the side, or get yanked to the bottom of the river. If you wait for the indicator to submerge, you will miss 50% of your takes.

The most important thing about an indicator is, obviously, that you can see it. Foam stick-ons, corkies, etc. are fine for short line situations but are useless for long drifts. The best and most versatile indicator yet devised is polypropylene yarn (macramé yarn). This stuff is cheap, comes in every color imaginable, can be trimmed to any size, and can be placed anywhere on the leader with a simple slip loop. Lime green is the best all around color for our light conditions. Reds and yellows are not good because light reflected off canyon walls is reddish. Black is the best in flat white glare. White is good in all conditions except flat white glare. Fluff the thing with a piece of Velcro (there is some somewhere on your vest), add a small bit of floatant, and you are set.

Eye Glasses

A good pair of polarized glasses is not an accessory at all, it is a necessity. One of the most rewarding possibilities at Lee's Ferry is the chance to spot, stalk and cast to a large rainbow. If you can't spot, you don't get a chance to stalk and cast. The high canyon walls reflect light and produce very glary conditions especially in late fall, winter, and early spring, when the sun is low in the sky. Polarized glasses should be comfortable all day and need a retention device to thwart loss. I prefer glass lenses, as they are nearly indestructible. While no single lens will cover all fishing situations, a copper or medium brown lens is most versatile. These colors increase contrast and are soothing to the eyes. In midwinter conditions, a yellow or amber lens helps increase contrast in the low light conditions prevalent on the Ferry at this time of year.

Split Shot Sizes			
Shown Actual Size			
●	SSG	•	4
●	AB	•	6
●	BB	•	8
•	1	•	10

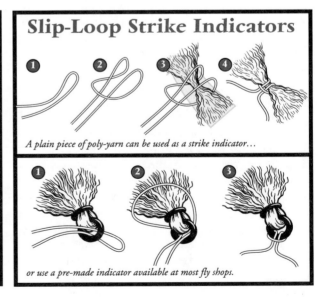

Slip-Loop Strike Indicators

A plain piece of poly-yarn can be used as a strike indicator…

or use a pre-made indicator available at most fly shops.

Conditions By The Month

December-February

Cold temperatures and spawning fish characterize December-January. By late November fish are usually moving into the shallows to spawn and large numbers of fish are usually in the shallows by December. Some of the largest fish of the year are caught during this time. Sight fishing using roe imitations, chironomids, scuds and annelids is the most productive method. Because of reduced sunlight in the canyon, invertebrate activity is reduced. This means feeding activity is reduced. Most productive periods are typically during rising water and when sunlight hits the river. Dry fly fishing is possible, but is typically limited to the back eddy scum lines. In the back eddies Parachute Adams, Griffith's Gnats and other midge imitations are effective. This is typically one of the least crowded times of the year.

March-May

Warming temperatures and increased sunlight mean an increase in midge activity. All areas of the river receive some sunlight by March 10. Feeding tempo increases dramatically during this time. When heavy midge hatches occur, the water column can be thick with drifting pupae. The Zebra Midge and all its variations are effective in this situation. This is the one time of year that fish sometimes feed heavily on emergers and adult midges in the riffles. Some spawning fish can still be found through the end of March. This is one of the most popular times to fish Lee's Ferry.

June-August

In most years, the average flow increases in June as power demands are increased. Fishing is sometimes off for a couple weeks following a large increase. Once things stabilize, the summer months provide the best dry fly fishing of the year at Lee's Ferry. Grasshoppers, ants, cicadas, spiders and beetles all become available to fish as higher water washes these insects into the river. Sinking lines and Woolly Buggers are also effective. The summer is less popular than other times and the river can provide a wonderfully uncrowded fishing experience.

September-November

The fall finds fish in peak condition. October 1 is the end of the water year for the Colorado River and in most years the average flow drops in October. This situation always improves the fishing for at least a couple of weeks. All the typical Lee's Ferry patterns and techniques are productive. Dry fly fishing tapers off in October. The exception is the back eddies which continue to provide dry fly fishing to smaller midging fish.

When conditions are just right, a tape measure is needed, too.

15

Unbelievable
Sizes #14-16

San Juan Worm
Sizes #12-18

Deer Hair Back Scud
Sizes #8-14

WD40
Sizes #18-24

Beadhead Zebra Midge
Sizes #16-22

Chironomids
Sizes #16-22

Glo Bug
Sizes #12-16

Midge Pupa
Sizes #16-22

Griffith's Gnat
Sizes #18-22

Parachute Adams
Sizes #14-22

Royal Wulff
Sizes #8-12

Humpy
Sizes #8-12

Dave's Hopper
Sizes #6-10

Stimulator
Sizes #6-10

Woolly Bugger
Sizes #4-8

Flies for Lee's Ferry

One of the most interesting aspects of fly fishing Lee's Ferry is the wide range of tactics and patterns that can be used. The primary food sources here are chironomid midges, scuds, aquatic annelids, roe and terrestrials. Many of these food sources are available to trout in two or three different forms or life stages. Therefore, various colors, sizes and types of flies are used, depending on the situation.

Dredge up a handful of algae and you're likely to see dozens of scuds (*Gammarus lacustris*) scurrying to get back into the river. These amphipods are a quarter to a half-inch long and are gray, olive or brown. They are a predominant trout food at Lee's Ferry. Often, when a two-fly nymph rig is used, one of the flies is a scud imitation. As most long time Lee's Ferry anglers understand, however, live scud imitations are not particularly effective. This is probably because live scuds are not easily available for trout to feed on. Scuds spend most of their lives burrowed deeply in moss and free float only occasionally during reproduction. It is during low flows that scuds become an important food source when they are exposed, die and change color to a pale orange or orangish-brown. Rising water then washes these morsels to waiting trout. The most popular patterns utilize synthetic dubbings such as Umpqua sparkle blends in pink, orange, ginger and squirrel belly colors. The traditional Lee's Ferry scud pattern is tied in sizes #14-18 with a deer hair back and fine copper wire ribbing.

Chironomid midges are another important food source at Lee's Ferry. Nearly forty species of these tiny insects have been identified and there are midge hatches almost every day of the year. Peak midge activity occurs in spring and early summer with a lesser peak in the winter months, when activity generally occurs only in areas that receive sunlight. During spring and summer, midge activity can occur all day long. With as many midge species as Lee's Ferry supports, there is a huge range of both size and color. To be successful, it helps to be observant and try to match the size, color and life stage characteristics as closely as possible. Most days, size is more important than color.

Chironomid midges have a four-stage life cycle. Midge larvae are thin, helpless worms with distinct body segmentation but no noticeable taper. They are found in a variety of colors including creamy white, gray, brown, pale olive and red. Popular imitations are tied by sliding Larva-Lace over a hook and then giving a ribbed appearance by wrapping thread lightly around the Larva-Lace. Simply wrapping a hook with thread in various colors also produces effective imitations.

When fully developed, midge larvae transform into midge pupae. During this stage, the appearance is changed to a shorter, more tapered shape with a pronounced thorax that contains the developing wings. Traditional patterns that effectively imitate this stage include the Beadhead Zebra Midge, Miracle Nymph and Yong Special. Variations in color, material and tying style are endless. This stage invites experimentation at the fly tying bench.

When conditions are right, the fully developed pupae will drift freely with the current. During heavy spring hatches, the water column can be especially thick with drifting pupae heading for the surface to become emergers. It is at times like these that the most intense feeding activity is often observed. Fish dart from side to side gorging themselves, sometimes suspended midway in the water column. Effective patterns are the WD-40 and RS2.

Because of the amount of energy used to chase down adult midges on the surface, this midge life stage is probably less important to Lee's Ferry trout than the previously mentioned stages. Adult midge imitations are still important. If fished in the proper area they produce when no other technique is effective. Generally, fish feed most heavily on adults where midges accumulate, such as the back eddies. In these areas the Griffith's Gnat, Renegade, Parachute Adams and other patterns that imitate a mass of midges are effective.

During the November through March spawning season, roe imitations are very effective. Generally use #16-20 Globug types. These in sizes #12-14 are also an effective spin fishing pattern. The most popular colors at Lee's Ferry are yellow, chartreuse, light pink, pink and roe. Usually they are finished with a red or orange dot in the middle of the fly.

This stretch of the Colorado also has an abundance of aquatic segmented worms. Imitate these with a #14-18 San Juan Worm pattern. The most popular colors are red, orange and a natural light brown.

No Lee's Ferry box would be complete without a good selection of traditional attractor and terrestrial patterns. Especially during the summer months, fish will often readily take large attractors and terrestrials. Effective patterns include Royal Wulffs, Irresistibles, Humpies, Stimulators and your favorite ant, hopper and cicada patterns. In the larger sizes, these types of flies also make excellent strike indicators when fishing dry fly and dropper rigs.

Sight fishing with a classic drag-free drift, mending to maintain a slack line. Photo by Dave Foster.

Techniques

The Lee's Ferry stretch of the Colorado River is a unique tailwater fishery unmatched in the variety of fishing situations. On one hand, it is probably the largest river most anglers will ever fish for trout. On the other, its clarity, consistent temperatures, and predominant food sources often create spring creek-like conditions. Virtually all fly fishing techniques can be used on this water at one time of the year or another. The key is matching the proper technique to the time of year, water level and fishing situation.

Nymph Fishing

Nymphing is undoubtedly the most consistent way to catch trout with a fly rod at Lee's Ferry. Although surface activity does occur in certain situations, Lee's Ferry rainbows do the majority of their feeding sub-surface on scuds, annelids and chironomids. The two most important aspects of nymph fishing are presenting the fly on a drag-free drift and getting the fly in front of the fish.

A drag-free drift is best described as presenting the fly at the exact speed as the water that surrounds it. This seems simple, but remember that the fly is attached to a leader, a flyline and an angler, all moving at different speeds from the water the fly is in. Therefore, it is necessary to manipulate the flyline to prevent it from influencing the drift of the fly. This manipulation is called mending and, depending on the situation, it is done in either an up-current or down-current direction. If the flyline is in water moving faster than the water the fly is in, the mend is made up-current to slow the speed of the line, otherwise the flyline pulls the fly. If the flyline is in water moving slower than the fly, the mend will be made down-current to allow the line to catch up with the fly, otherwise the line unnaturally slows the fly. Additionally, if a cast is made at an upstream angle, the flyline has a head start on the fly and will eventually drag the fly in an unnatural manner. If an upstream cast is made, it is usually followed by an upstream mend.

Because of the size, temperature and velocity of the Colorado River, Lee's Ferry rainbows will not usually move a great distance to feed. The fly must be presented in front of the fish. Think about it. If a trout expended twice as many calories chasing down a tiny chironomid as it got from consuming it, we would soon have no trout. I tell my beginning anglers that trout live in a 12"x12" box and the fly has to be in that box. One of the most common mistakes is not rigging and presenting the fly in a manner that delivers it to the proper depth, inside the fish's "box". Keep in mind the three factors that influence nymph depth: 1) length of leader, 2) amount of weight added to the leader, and 3) the duration of the drift.

For Lee's Ferry nymphing, use a leader one and one-half to two times the depth of the water. This extra length is needed because a fly does not sink straight down, but travels at an angle. A typical nymphing rig includes a point fly and a dropper fly. The dropper is attached to either the eye or the bend of the hook. It is usually 12" long and a split shot is placed 12" above the point fly. You can use too long a leader too. This makes the rig hard to cast and increases the time it takes for a strike to be transmitted and detected, allowing the fish more time to get rid of the fly.

Although it seems obvious, adding the proper amount of weight to the leader, and taking time to adjust it, is often overlooked. Carry a good selection of shot; sizes #6, #4, #1 and #BB is not overkill. With

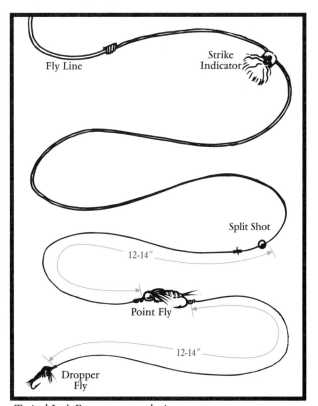

Fly Line

Strike Indicator

Split Shot

12-14"

Point Fly

12-14"

Dropper Fly

Typical Lee's Ferry two-nymph rig.

these you can fine tune the amount of weight it takes to nymph at the right depth. A good rule is to try to hit the bottom every four or five drifts. If you don't, and you aren't hooking fish, add weight.

The duration of the drift is really the most flexible aspect of all this, because it can be adjusted every cast. The concept is simple: cast far enough up current of the target zone to allow time for the fly to get to the proper depth. Don't simply cast at fish you can see, the nymph will drift over the top of the fish and be outside of that box. To apply this idea, first identify the target zone, perhaps a fish you can see, a drop off, or just an area you think holds a fish. Then calculate how far *ahead* of the target the fly must land in order to sink to the proper depth. Consider depth, water velocity, and the weight added to the leader. During successive casts, make adjustments either closer to or further upstream of the target to get the fly presented at just the right depth.

Extended Drift Nymphing Equals Success at Lee's Ferry

Much of this stretch of the Colorado is characterized by broad, open riffles that are fairly deep and have uniform current speed. These areas present perfect conditions for deep water extended drift nymph fishing. This method is the logical alternative to short-line or

Shaking out fly line to achieve an extended drag-free drift. Photo by Dave Foster.

"high sticking" methods which achieve a drag free drift by limiting the amount of flyline on the water. In extended drift nymphing, extremely long drag free drifts are accomplished through the control and manipulations of the flyline. This method allows the fly to sink to the proper depth and then maximizes the amount of time the fly spends at that depth. It also allows you to cover large stretches of water.

The technique is simple, but requires a bit of coordination. The cast is made up-current at something close

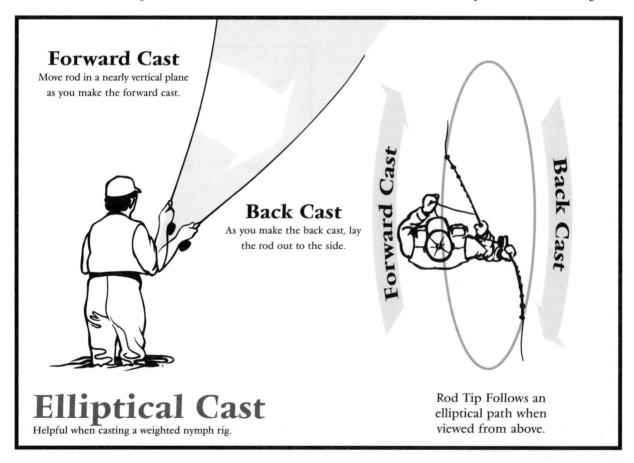

Forward Cast
Move rod in a nearly vertical plane as you make the forward cast.

Back Cast
As you make the back cast, lay the rod out to the side.

Forward Cast

Back Cast

Elliptical Cast
Helpful when casting a weighted nymph rig.

Rod Tip Follows an elliptical path when viewed from above.

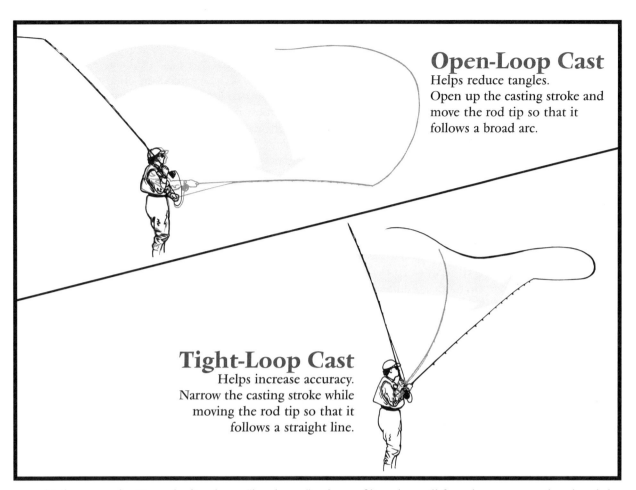

Open-Loop Cast
Helps reduce tangles.
Open up the casting stroke and move the rod tip so that it follows a broad arc.

Tight-Loop Cast
Helps increase accuracy. Narrow the casting stroke while moving the rod tip so that it follows a straight line.

to a 45-degree angle. Since the line has a "head start" on the fly, an upstream mend is made. Using a reach cast will make large mends more manageable. Now, as the fly drifts to a point in front of you, extend your line control hand, (the one not holding the rod), out to the side, allowing line to slide through it. At full extension, grip the line and shake the rod tip vigorously from side to side. As the line is shaken out of the tip of the rod, bring the line control hand back in towards your body at the same rate as the line leaves the tip. Pull more line off the water, and repeat at a rate that allows the drift to continue drag free.

A few tips. First, when you slide the line control hand down the line to retrieve the next length of line, get as much as possible. The more line you get, the fewer times you will have to go through this maneuver. Second, the key to hooking fish is to be in the ready position. That is, with the line in the index finger of your rod hand and your line hand holding the line right next to it. You'll want to "strip strike" by making a big strip with the line hand as the rod is raised sharply up over your head. Try to spend as much time in this ready position as possible. Shake the line out as quickly and efficiently as you can and get the line back behind the index finger of the rod hand. Lastly, after reaching back and grabbing the line to be shaken out, do not move the line hand forward and then try to shake line. The

loop of line that will form between your hand and the stripping guide (the first guide on the rod) will flip up and over the rod, making it impossible to efficiently feed line out. The line hand should come forward at the same rate the line leaves the rod tip. This technique takes time to master but is well worth the effort!

Help Casting A Weighted Rig

Let's face it, casting split shot and long leaders is a pain for most anglers and many refuse to even try. Some go so far as to claim that this is not fly fishing. While we won't get into the ethical debate here, to be effective in the wide range of conditions presented on this river you should master the technique. A couple of simple methods help:

First, power up. Put enough into both the backcast and the forecast to keep the added mass of the split shot in the air. Delicacy is not a factor in this situation. If enough power is not used on the backcast, the leader will not straighten out behind you and the rod will not be properly loaded.

Second, slow down. To the uninitiated this may seem contrary to the first tip, but you need to wait for the backcast to fully extend before beginning the forecast. If you don't, tension will be taken off the leader and the rig will fall out of the air.

Lastly, open up your loop. Throwing a wider, more

open loop will reduce tangles. To do this, simply bring the rod tip slightly lower on the forecast. It will also help if you throw a slightly elliptical loop into your cast. Cock your wrist and arm to the side as you make your backcast. The loop will then form horizontally, rather than vertically. On the forecast, bring your rod tip back towards your body. From above, the rod tip appears to travel in an oval, or ellipse (see diagram, page 20).

Shallow Water Nymphing
Dry Fly and Dropper

Shallow water nymphing techniques can be utilized anywhere fish are holding near the surface or will come to within two to three feet of the surface to take a nymph. This situation may occur along the shallow margins of bars or in deep water that is quite slow. Less weight and shorter leaders make these rigs far easier to cast and are well suited for beginning flycasters.

Shallow water tactics are most effective in two situations. When rising water washes over a bar exposed the night before, extremely vigorous feeding can occur in the shallows just below the bar. Often this is in inches of water. Also, in the deeper, slower water of back eddies or deep runs, fish hold and feed a few feet below the surface, well off the bottom. Here, because of slower currents, fish can expend a little energy to hold in the middle of the water column or travel three to four feet to take a tiny midge.

A dry fly and dropper rig is an effective way to fish these situations. This consists of a buoyant dry fly such as an Irresistible, Stimulator, Unbelievable or Humpy with a nymph suspended on two to four feet of tippet beneath it. Typically, a beadhead or weighted nymph is used. Tie the tippet on the nymph and then at either the bend or the eye of the dry fly hook. This makes the dry fly a very sensitive and effective strike indicator as well as a possible target.

Dry Fly Fishing

Although Lee's Ferry is not known as a dry fly fishery, the opportunity to successfully fish dries is available every day of the year if you look in the right areas and utilize the proper techniques and patterns. If you encounter the right conditions, you can have spectacular surface action.

One of these situations is associated with the daily fluctuations in releases from the dam. As the water rises, it carries dead scuds and other invertebrates which float. Fish move into very shallow water around the margins of gravel bars to get to this food. The fishing can be furious until the food is gone or until the water becomes so deep that fish are less willing to travel to the surface. This is exactly the situation for which the Unbelievable fly was developed. This unusual pattern imitates dead, dry, orange scuds. Also try attractors such as the Humpy, Royal Wulff, Stimulator, Irresistible and Adams.

Midges hatch every day of the year at Lee's Ferry and some days these hatches are almost beyond belief. The subsurface life stages of these tiny insects are one of the most important food sources for our trout. In the right conditions, however, trout will feed voraciously on winged adults at the surface. One area where fish consistently feed on midges is in the back eddies. Here, huge numbers of adult midges, midge shucks and other debris is accumulated by re-circulating currents. These are commonly referred to as "scum lines" and most are in deep water and must be fished from an anchored boat. If you approach carefully, dozens of noses can be seen just breaking the surface as fish "slurp" clumps of midges. Though feeding is often vigorous, careful placement of the fly is needed to keep from putting the fish down. If this occurs, wait a few minutes. They will be back soon. Use individual midge patterns, though clump patterns such as Griffith's Gnat or Parachute Adams are equally as effective and easier to see.

In the slower shallow riffles and runs, fish will sometimes rise to individual adult midges or emergers. Casting to these fish is probably the most frustrating and difficult Lee's Ferry fly fishing. It can also be one of the most rewarding if you enjoy technical sight fishing. A two to four weight rod is ideal for these situations, and a twelve foot leader with 7x-8x tippet is sometimes necessary. Limit your targets to rhythmically and consistently rising fish. Sporadic risers are generally a waste of time. Because the flies are almost impossible to see, learn to place a fly within a dinner plate sized area and then strike on any fish rising in this area. This type of midge fishing is more common in the spring when a couple of varieties of larger midges often show up.

At all times of the year, but especially in the summer, fish may be taken on large attractors and terrestrials. Cicadas, hoppers, ants and beetles become available as rising water washes them into the river. This is one of the few instances when fish might move a great distance to take a dry fly. During the summer, casting from a drifting boat towards vegetation-covered banks is a pleasant departure from the usual Lee's Ferry tactics. Sometimes, the bigger and uglier the fly, the better!

Sight Fishing

By far one of the most exciting aspects of fly fishing Lee's Ferry is the opportunity to spot, stalk and cast to a large fish. Crystal clear water and broad open riffles provide some of the best sight fishing opportunities available anywhere. Nurture just a few skills and techniques and you will enjoy success in the shallows.

First, learn to spot fish. It goes without saying that you'll need a good pair of polarized sunglasses. (Suggestions are in the gear section.) Good glasses don't necessarily make seeing fish easy and sometimes the worst way to approach the challenge is to look for a fish. Instead, train yourself to look for an aspect or characteristic of a fish. Usually you will spot something like a bright red gill plate on a spawning fish, or the fish's shadow in a brightly-lit run. Sometimes the fish's tail is the most visible body part. The other thing to look for is an aberration in the color and texture of the river bottom. Use your peripheral vision when scanning an area. Look for a gray or silvery green patch that may not stand out when you stare directly at it. This might be your trout. Now use your mind's eye to fill in other details and suddenly, boom, there is a trout lying right in front of you. Another good trick is to look for windows in the surface of the water. Patches of water with a smooth surface and less distortion continually pass by. Learn to spot these windows and follow them downstream, scanning as you go. If you see something that looks like a fish, lock your eyes on it, waiting for a little movement that gives it away. A variation on this occurs when boats come past. When the wake rolls in, the surface of the water tilts, allowing a clearer view of the bottom.

Once spotted, the challenge is to get the fly to the fish. Remember, these fish live in a 12"x12" box, and your fly has to be in the box. Generally, the best position for casting is just a little upstream of your target, provided, of course, lighting conditions cooperate. If you can't see, move to a position where you can. Cast to a point upstream of the fish that allows the nymph to sink to the proper depth. When the nymph hits the water, follow this water (that contains the nymph) downstream to the target. Look for the fish's mouth to open or a movement straight back or to the side. When the fish reverses this movement to move back to its lie, lift up. At this instant the fish either has taken the fly or has refused it and is heading back to its lie. Either way, it will be time to lift up and play a fish or cast again.

Spin Fishing

With the proper tackle, spin fishing can be every bit as productive and rewarding as fly fishing at Lee's Ferry. Typically, spin fishing is from a boat and is approached three ways: drift fishing with flies or rubber worms, casting and retrieving spoons, spinners, plugs and jigs, or back trolling diving lures. With all these methods the lure must be presented near the bottom. All lures are required to be barbless and it is a good idea to cut off one hook from each treble hook on a lure. You won't lose any fish and this practice makes releasing them far easier. It will also prevent mortally hooking a fish in the eye or deep into the body.

Drift fishing is probably the most popular way to spin fish at the Ferry. Use small rubber worms, Globugs, Woolly Worm flies or other fly patterns and pencil lead attached with surgical tubing. Place the weight about 3 feet above the "bait". Usually the best areas for this type of fishing have consistent slow to moderate currents. This is important because, to achieve a good drift, the boat should not be in water moving at a significantly different speed than the water you are fishing. The boat is drifted bow upstream and the cast is made perpendicular to the boat. Sink the rig to the bottom where it can bounce along. A little practice is required to tell a take from a "bottom bump". Beginners should be aggressive and strike on anything that feels unusual. Generally, this method is best on rising water when there is a lot of food in the drift.

Using one-eighth-ounce jigs of black, brown or orange marabou is another very productive method. Different water conditions may call for one-quarter or one-sixteenth-ounce lures. An ultra-light rod equipped with four-pound test line helps cast these lighter lures and also helps detect subtle takes. If drifting, cast perpendicular to the boat. From an anchored boat cast into an eddy. Let the lure sink and then make four to five fast cranks with the rod tip high. Stop, let the jig sink and then repeat. The take often comes as the jig sinks and is betrayed by a "collapsing" of the arc of line going from the rod tip to the water. It takes a little practice to see this change in the line, but this is a very effective method. At other times, try three or four jerks with the rod tip, followed by a retrieve. Jig fishing is especially good during periods of low or non-fluctuating flows when there is less drifting food.

Back trolling involves a diving lure, one with some sort of lip that drives the lure to the bottom. Cast to the side of a boat (with the motor running) and let the lure swing around downstream of the boat without retrieving. The boat drifts downstream, but at a speed slower than the current. This acts the same as if you are retrieving the diving lure and drives it to the bottom, where it hovers. Then back the boat down the river, working the lure through likely holes. Back troll only in areas where the boat will not obstruct a drifting boat. A boat not under power has the right of way.

Anglers fishing the crystal clear riffle at Mile 13, not quite 100 feet apart, but they are close friends. Photo by Dave Foster.

Etiquette

In 1992, when the first edition of this book was published, there was no need for a section on river etiquette. There just weren't that many people fly fishing Lee's Ferry. Today it is one of the most popular destinations in the West and on some days is in danger of becoming over-crowded. This is compounded by the fact that, for a river its size and length, there is relatively little productive fly fishing water. Shallow gravel bars and riffles, the most productive fly fishing water, are not continuous but are interspersed along the river. Between these areas are stretches of deep water. Often a cliff face falls directly into the river, making the area unsuitable for fly fishing. Anglers target and congregate in specific areas and crowding is compounded. At certain water flows or certain seasons, some bars fish significantly better than others and, of course, everyone wants to fish these bars. Here are a few guidelines that help assure everyone enjoys their experience at the Ferry. Some are common sense and universal, others are particular to Lee's Ferry. The underlying principle is the old standard, "Do unto others as you would have them do unto you."

1. First Come, First Served. This is the most basic principle of etiquette at Lee's Ferry and has been practiced here for as long as the fishery has existed. If there is a boat on a bar you want to fish, go somewhere else. This holds even if the angler parked 100 yards from the best water or in some non-standard parking area. It applies even if nobody is fishing when you pull up. Maybe a knot-tying lesson is underway or maybe they stopped fishing for an early lunch.

2. Courteous Communication. When it seems your only chance to fly fish is, say, an occupied 100 yard long gravel bar, simply ask first. If you can, turn off your motor, drift by at a courteous distance and yell, "Mind if I fish the lower part of this bar?" If it is a noisy riffle and you have to pull in and walk up – without out a rod in hand – do that. Just make sure you don't drive your boat through some fishable water. The safest bet is to park right next to the other party's boat. If the other boat is where it should be, all is well. If the other boat is in the middle of the best riffle, the damage has already been done.

3. One Hundred Foot Rule. OK, you pulled in on another angler, are courteous, and the guy says, "Sure, come on in, there's plenty of room". Just how close should you get to that area where he is nailing fish after fish? It depends on the riffle, but a good rule of thumb is 100 feet. Much of the nymph fishing here involves an extended drift of more than fifty-sixty feet downstream of where you are standing. A flyline is typically ninety feet long and this guy might be fishing every inch of it, so watch how he is fishing and don't interfere. If in doubt, stay at least 100 feet away.

4. No Dropping Off. Some boaters drop an angler or two off at a bar and then head off with the boat to occupy another location. This is increasingly common and is both discourteous and dangerous. With increased use, it is simply not fair for a single group to occupy more than one location. A few of the more popular fishing areas have troughs that can be waded at low water but become hazardous as the water rises. You can be stranded on the wrong side of such a trough and get into serious trouble without a boat to help. If you engage in this practice, expect unpleasant encounters with other anglers and guides.

A few years ago Al Kyte, in an article in *California Flyfisher*, summed it up best.

"As I continue to pick my way along trout waters, I believe I will make better use of a smile, nod and even a brief chat. I will continue to give other anglers the space I would like them to give me. If I observe a breach of etiquette, I will try to offer advice in as friendly and suggestive a manner as possible. I will make an effort to see my fellow angler as a friend I haven't met rather than as a rival for the same fish."

Shuffling

In the past few years, a "technique" has come into use by some that is both unethical and destructive. Shuffling is the intentional disruption of the river bottom in order to attract fish and stimulate them into feeding activity. Basically, it is chumming. It is an extremely harmful practice that both destroys aquatic habitat and eventually conditions fish to come to a wading angler's feet. The practice is illegal in many states. At Lee's Ferry, it can be considered habitat destruction within a National Recreation Area.

Shuffling is analogous to hunting deer over a salt lick. Conscientious and ethical anglers don't fish this way. If you witness anglers vigorously moving their feet to dislodge vegetation and fishing directly below themselves in the chum line, take the time to explain why this is not a practice conscientious anglers employ.

Unintentional shuffling can also be detrimental. Some bars are shallow enough to allow you to wade out into heavy current. Fish will move near your feet to take advantage of the food you kick up and the current break you create. These fish, pulled from their natural lies, are out of the group of trout to be fished conventionally. They will continue to hold at your feet until you move out of the current. Try to limit wading into riffles. If you feel you need to reach further out, make longer casts. The truth is, most fish hold on the inside margins of riffles where the current is reduced. Most guides will tell you that a common mistake newcomers make is wading out into the spot they should fish.

Guide Barbara Foster and client with a beautiful 18" rainbow at Eight Mile Bar. Photo by Scott Baxter.

Hiring a Lee's Ferry Guide

If you don't have a boat, hiring a guide is the only way to easily fish the fifteen mile stretch of river between Glen Canyon dam and Lee's Ferry. There are about forty licensed guides currently on this stretch of river. The United States Coast Guard, the Arizona Department of Game and Fish and The National Parks Service license them all. For the first-timer, a guide is an invaluable resource that can add a great deal of enjoyment and education. Here are a few suggestions to make the most of a guided trip.

Keep an Open Mind

Remember that a fishing guide is an expert on the piece of water you are visiting. Leave your preconceived notions in the car and be open to any suggestions the guide may have. On the Colorado, we often employ tactics foreign to many of our visitors. Enjoy the education. I have often said that guiding is really only an exercise in balancing expectations with reality. Sometimes this is easy, other times it is impossible. The more open-minded a client, the easier it is for everyone to have a great day.

Speak Your Mind

If there is something you would like to do or try, let the guide know. Guides may be experts at fishing the river, but they are not mind readers. A good guide is accommodating and will fulfill your wishes but will also, if necessary, explain the limitations of a particular technique. For example, you may say, "I only want to fish dry flies". A good guide will point out that Lee's Ferry is not a particularly consistent dry fly fishery, ex-cept under certain conditions in certain areas. This explained, the guide will allow the client to call it from there. A guide should not allow the angler to fish for an hour before letting him know the technique he insists on using can't possibly work with the current river conditions or location.

Be Prepared
or Let the Guide Know You Aren't

To get the most out of a trip, do a little homework. This might mean a casting lesson at your local shop or ten minutes of daily casting practice the week before the trip. While guides generally don't mind teaching beginners to cast, casting is something that can be learned in the backyard. Fishing, not casting, is what you need a river for and you will get the most out of your time with a guide if you can concentrate on advanced skills. If you are a beginner and show up cold, let the guide know. This influences where he decides to fish and how he approaches the day.

Taking a quick nap between fish. Photo by Dave Foster.

Springtime at Eight Mile Bar. Can you find the angler? Photo by Dave Foster.

Weather and Climate

T he climate of the Lee's Ferry area is continental and arid and the weather is highly variable. Lee's Ferry regularly experiences an annual temperature range of 100 degrees. It averages fifty-eight days a year with a high temperature of 100 degrees or more and eighty-four days a year with a minimum temperature of 32 degrees or less. Average annual precipitation is 5.8 inches, with most rain occurring during the summer "monsoon" season. Record temperatures at Lee's Ferry were 115 degrees in June of 1954 and 3 degrees in January of 1963.

	High Temp	Low Temp	Precip.		High Temp	Low Temp	Precip.
Jan	47.8	25.8	0.37	**Jul**	103.1	72.3	0.73
Feb	56.8	31.9	0.42	**Aug**	99.7	69.9	1.04
Mar	66.4	38.8	0.48	**Sep**	92.8	61.3	0.52
Apr	76.9	47.3	0.37	**Oct**	78.3	47.5	0.59
May	86.8	56.2	0.29	**Nov**	61.1	34.7	0.45
Jun	97.7	64.7	0.21	**Dec**	48.9	26.7	0.46

Average monthly high and low temperatures in degrees Fahrenheit and average precipitation in inches at Lee's Ferry. Records from April 1916 to December 1982.

Spring
March 22 - June 21

Spring brings an irregular warming trend and unpredictable weather to Lee's Ferry. Moisture-laden Pacific storms become less frequent. Throughout the spring, the area is buffeted by unbelievably relentless and powerful winds. Tumbleweeds float hundreds of feet above the canyon floor. Boaters know that these high winds can produce unsafe boating conditions. By late June, temperatures can approach 100 degrees.

Summer
June 22 - September 21

Daytime highs are often over 100 degrees. The summer rainy season begins in mid-July. Moist oceanic air is drawn up from the south. Intense solar heating during the day produces thermal uplifting and creates spectacular thunderheads which, by early afternoon, can produce rain and hail at rates of several inches an hour. These rainstorms often produce spectacular waterfalls throughout Glen Canyon and may temporarily muddy the river above Lee's Ferry. High humidity and cooler morning temperatures at this time of year can create a band of fog several feet thick on the river's surface. While beautiful, this makes for hazardous boating.

Fall
September 22 - December 21

Weather becomes progressively cooler and drier. Pacific storms increase and the first frost of the year is normally around the last week of October.

Winter
December 22 - March 21

Weather becomes increasingly unstable. Winter storms can bring rain and snow although snow rarely sticks at river level. The surrounding cliffs may be white for weeks at a time during the coldest months. Daily highs rise to the 40's or 50's, although shady portions of the canyon may remain below freezing all day.

View looking downstream from above Lee's Ferry. The gravel bar on the right was formed by the Paria River. This bar is known as "the walk-in area" and is the best area accessible to anglers without a boat. Photo by Dave Foster.

Water Levels and Flows

The single most important influence on the Lee's Ferry fishery is the flow regime from Glen Canyon Dam. Until the early 1990's, daily flows were based entirely on the demand for hydroelectric power. The dam was operated as a "peaking power" or "load following" facility. Releases varied greatly throughout the day and the seasons as demands for electricity grew or subsided. Flows could vary as much as 15,000 cubic feet per second (cfs) in a single day. Concern over the impact of such flow regimes on downstream resources led to a series of studies that began in 1982. These studies showed that release characteristics, including ramping rates (the rate water rises or drops) and the magnitude of high and low flows had a dramatic impact on the downstream riparian habitats and the native species in Grand Canyon National Park. Beginning in the early 1990's, regulations sought to minimize flow related impacts to the ecosystems in Grand Canyon. As of this writing, daily flow patterns for Glen Canyon Dam are as follows:

Maximum release: 25,000 cfs.
Minimum release: 5,000 cfs.
Maximum change in 24 hours: 8,000 cfs.
Up-ramp limit: 4,000 cfs an hour.
Down-ramp limit: 2,500 cfs an hour.

Flows outside these parameters are implemented in special situations. For instance, experimental releases based on pre-dam flow patterns are used to benefit native fishes in the Grand Canyon. Also, as a hydroelectric facility, Glen Canyon Dam is occasionally called upon to fill unexpected or emergency power demands.

Flow Changes

Daily and seasonal flow variations have a dramatic bearing on fishing conditions. Generally, the lower the water, the better the fishing. The "container" is smaller and fish are more condensed. Fish and fishable areas are also more accessible. At low flows (5,000-9,000 cfs) and medium flows (10,000-16,000 cfs) there are many more exposed gravel bars and much more topography to the river than at high flows (17,000-25,000 cfs). More riffles and seams mean more holding water. At flows of over 25,000 cfs most areas of the river become difficult to fish with a fly rod.

Seasonal

Significant changes from an established pattern of flow can influence fishing conditions. These changes occur fall and spring, or (seemingly at random) for increased power generation or to benefit downstream resources. Generally, major changes occur in October when the water drops and in May or June when flows increase to create hydroelectric power. Flow patterns, however, can change any month of the year. Flows decreasing from an established pattern generally improve the fishing. Fish move out of what was holding water (now dry land) and are condensed in the first new holding water they come to. Fishing may be excellent for a couple of weeks following such a change. The inverse is also true. An increase in average daily flows tends to disperse fish, spreading them throughout a given run. The newly flooded margins of the river are devoid of aquatic vegetation and fish are naturally slow to move into these areas. Keep in mind the general rule of thumb regarding changes in seasonal flow patterns at Lee's Ferry. *The smaller the difference between the average high and the average low over a given period, the better the fishing and health of the fishery.*

Daily

Daily flow patterns are superimposed onto these seasonal patterns. Business power demands dictate that flows normally begin to increase between 5:00 a.m. and 7:00 a.m. and continue for two to four hours. Rising water washes stranded invertebrates off gravel bars and stimulates midge hatches. Fish feed vigorously during this time. During periods of high water (17,000-25,000 cfs) this rising water is almost certainly the best fishing of the day. Inversely, falling water tends to put fish off and feeding activity subsides.

Average daily high flows tend to be greater on weekdays and lesser on holidays and weekends. If you are camping, avoid getting beached. Anchor far offshore on Friday night. Flows for the next two days may not be enough to float your boat. It also means that Monday mornings often provide excellent fishing when flows increase more than in the previous two days.

Significant short-lived changes to established flow patterns can occasionally produce the most spectacular fishing you will ever experience. When the average low drops by a couple of thousand cubic feet per second, lots of river bottom is exposed and huge numbers of invertebrates are killed. When the water comes up again, these bugs and such are washed back into the river and the frenzy begins. If you are lucky enough to be on the river when this situation occurs, relish it as the once-in-a-lifetime fishing experience it is.

Midge
Adult

Midge
Pupa

Scud
(Gammarus)

Midge
Larva

Cladophora
glomerata

Diatoms

The Aquatic Ecosystem

With the construction of Glen Canyon dam the river ecosystems were forever and irreversibly changed. Today the river supports pre-dam species tolerant of post-dam conditions and a host of recent colonizers. Management agencies struggle to protect pre-dam environments and species, as required by law, and provide electric power and recreation. Stuck in the middle, and oblivious to this struggle, are the organisms that now inhabit the river.

The dam provides cooler water temperatures and less suspended sediment. Less sediment allows more sunlight to penetrate the water, which causes a dramatic increase in aquatic vegetation and the overall biomass of the system. This is especially dramatic in the Lee's Ferry reach where the water is consistently very clear. Biological productivity drops off dramatically downstream of Lee's Ferry where flooding from side streams clouds the river.

Diatoms, single-celled algae, are at the bottom of the Lee's Ferry food web. There are approximately 250 species of these tiny plants in the Colorado River and they are an important food source for fish and macro invertebrates. *Cladophora glomerata*, an attached filamentous green algae common in tailwaters, became the dominant Lee's Ferry aquatic vegetation by 1981. (Gosse, 1981) The aquatic macrophytes *Chara contraria* and *Potamogeton pectinatus* became co-dominant with *Cladophora* by 1996. New species continue to become established in the ever-evolving tailwater environment.

All these vegetation types provide important habitat and food for both the invertebrate and vertebrate species of the river. The diatoms use this vegetation as a substrate and are, in turn, grazed upon voraciously by *Gammarus lacustris* (scuds). This amphipod, often mistakenly referred to as freshwater shrimp, was introduced to the Colorado River drainage at Bright Angel Creek in 1932. After the closing of the dam, the Arizona Department of Game and Fish reintroduced *Gammarus* to the Lee's Ferry stretch, along with a host of other organisms including mayflies, snails, leeches, crayfish and at least ten families of aquatic insects from the San Juan River. Most did not survive, and *Gammarus*, along with Chironomid midges and segmented worms, are currently the most important food sources for the rainbow trout. Originally introduced in 1966-1967, Chironomid midges have only shown up as an important food source since the late 1980's. (Maddux, et. al., 1987) Species diversity and numbers increased with the relative stabilization of the river in the early 1990's, with nearly forty species of these tiny insects identified at various times of the year. The most prolific midge hatches generally occur in the spring and early summer, with a lesser peak in mid-winter. On the other hand, *Gammarus* increase in importance as a food source during the summer and fall. (McKinney and Persons, 1999)

The post-dam river has proven to be an ideal habitat for rainbow trout, which were planted at Lee's Ferry May, 1963. The early plantings, a hodge-podge of genetic strains and species, were based largely on the availability of healthy, low cost eggs. Little consideration was given to suitability for the Lee's Ferry environment, for instance, the same month the first rainbows were introduced, one million bass were planted. The bass didn't do well as river temperatures dropped. Silver salmon were planted once, and 508,000 brook trout were planted from 1978 to 1987. A state record brook trout, over five pounds, was caught at Lee's Ferry, although Brookies are a very unlikely catch today. From 1978 to 1980, 6,000 cutthroat trout were planted, though rainbows are by far the most successful game fish. In the 1970's and early 1980's the river yielded numerous trout over ten pounds and a few monsters approaching twenty pounds! The high water years of 1983 and 1984, with flows up to 92,600 cfs, displaced trout and scoured aquatic vegetation. When the flows returned to normal, the monsters were all but gone. A hot debate among anglers at Lee's Ferry is why we no longer see fish growing to these sizes. While there is no clear answer, it is probably a combination of factors such as genetic strain, population density, water nutrients and temperature.

Widely fluctuating flows in the 70's and 80's also stranded redds and dried out eggs. Adult fish and fry were killed and natural reproduction success was low, about 30%. In the early 1990's, naturally reproduced fish began to rival hatchery fish, and stocking programs were reduced. Since 1995, wild spawned trout account for 80% to 90% of the total population at Lee's Ferry. (Reger, et al, 1997) Today Lee's Ferry is managed as a trophy trout fishery with special regulations. It seems to be working. As of 2002, over 20,000 anglers a year come from around the world to sample one of the best trout fisheries in the west. Stabilized flows have turned what was essentially a put-and-take fishery into a self-sustaining wild trout fishery.

Lee's Ferry is the starting point for all raft trips through the Grand Canyon. The first take-out point is 225 miles downstream, and trip lengths average seven days for motorized trips and thirteen days for oar-powered trips. The Grand Canyon is considered one of the greatest whitewater river trips in the world. Photo by Dave Foster.

Lee's Ferry
River Miles

Directions in the text referring to the maps in this section are given facing upstream. North orientation on the maps changes from map to map (see the legend on each map). Maps "tile" from river mile to river mile with the match lines. River miles start at Mile Zero at Lee's Ferry and go upstream to Mile Fifteen at Glen Canyon Dam. Navigational hazards and spawning bars can change. Hazards and bars noted on these maps provide a general reference but are no substitute for boater caution and a qualified, licensed guide.

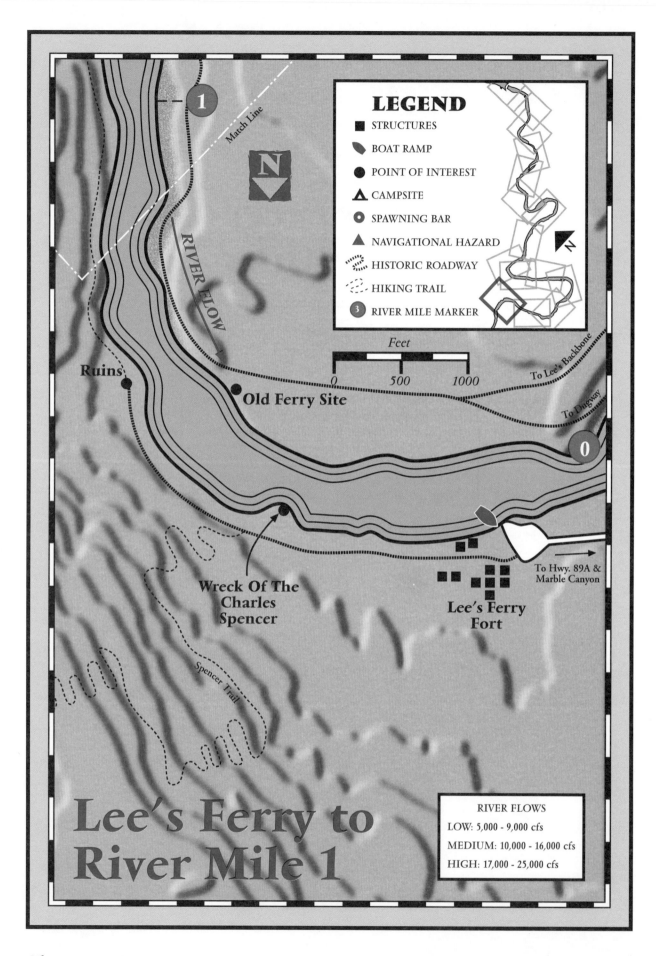

LEGEND

- ■ STRUCTURES
- ▮ BOAT RAMP
- ● POINT OF INTEREST
- ▲ CAMPSITE
- ◉ SPAWNING BAR
- ▲ NAVIGATIONAL HAZARD
- ⋯⋯ HISTORIC ROADWAY
- ⋯⋯ HIKING TRAIL
- ③ RIVER MILE MARKER

N

Match Line

RIVER FLOW

Feet

| 0 | 500 | 1000 |

To Lee's Backbone

To Dugway

Ruins

Old Ferry Site

0

Wreck Of The
Charles
Spencer

Spencer Trail

To Hwy. 89A &
Marble Canyon

Lee's Ferry
Fort

Lee's Ferry to
River Mile 1

RIVER FLOWS	
LOW: 5,000 - 9,000 cfs	
MEDIUM: 10,000 - 16,000 cfs	
HIGH: 17,000 - 25,000 cfs	

Mile 0

A wakeless zone extends from the dock to the upstream buoys. Boaters are prohibited below the downstream cable. A bed of Shinarump conglomerate juts steeply from the river opposite the boat ramp and slightly downstream. This is Lee's Backbone. From 1873 to 1898, a road atop it provided access from the south to the upper ferry site. The Dugway road, finished in 1898, parallels the river on the cliff face opposite the mouth of the Paria River. This road allowed travelers to trade a toilsome trip over "the Backbone" for a precipitous trip over the one-lane road a hundred feet above the river.

Mile .4

The wreckage of the Charles H. Spencer is on the left bank. In 1911, the steamboat was shipped from San Francisco in several pieces. It was to carry coal from Warm Creek (28 miles upstream) to a gold mining operation at Lee's Ferry. It cost $30,000, was 87 feet long, and was named for the engineer in charge of American Placer Corporation's operation at Lee's Ferry.

Mile .6

Look for cables from the ferry on the right bank, and a road leading to the ferry landing. Track cables were installed in 1896 while James Emett was ferry operator. Before this time, the ferry master simply rowed passengers across the river. An inscription, "SELMA 1923," is visible on a large boulder just below the ferry site and approximately fifty feet above river level. Many other inscriptions are nearby. On the left bank note the ruins of a way station used by early ferry travelers.

Mile .65

Hunting and loaded firearms are not permitted from this point downstream.

Mile .8

On the right, for approximately one and a half miles, is a road built in 1899 by mining engineer Robert Brewster Stanton. Stanton is best known as the leader of the second group to complete a river trip through Grand Canyon. He returned to Glen Canyon to operate the Hoskaninni Mining Company from 1897-1902. The company laid claim to 162 miles of Glen Canyon and intended to dredge the entire river bottom. To this end they brought in a 105 foot long floating dredge. Stanton's road was built as assessment work was required to keep the mining claims valid.

The most conspicuous historic building at Lee's Ferry is the Lee's Ferry Fort, built in 1874 under orders from Mormon leader Brigham Young. Used as a trading post into the 1880's, the fort later saw use as a mess hall during Spencer's mining operation. Photo by Dave Foster.

Stanton and crew enjoying Christmas Dinner, 1889. The menu included Colorado River salmon, probably Colorado River pike minnow. Photo courtesy of Utah State Historical Society.

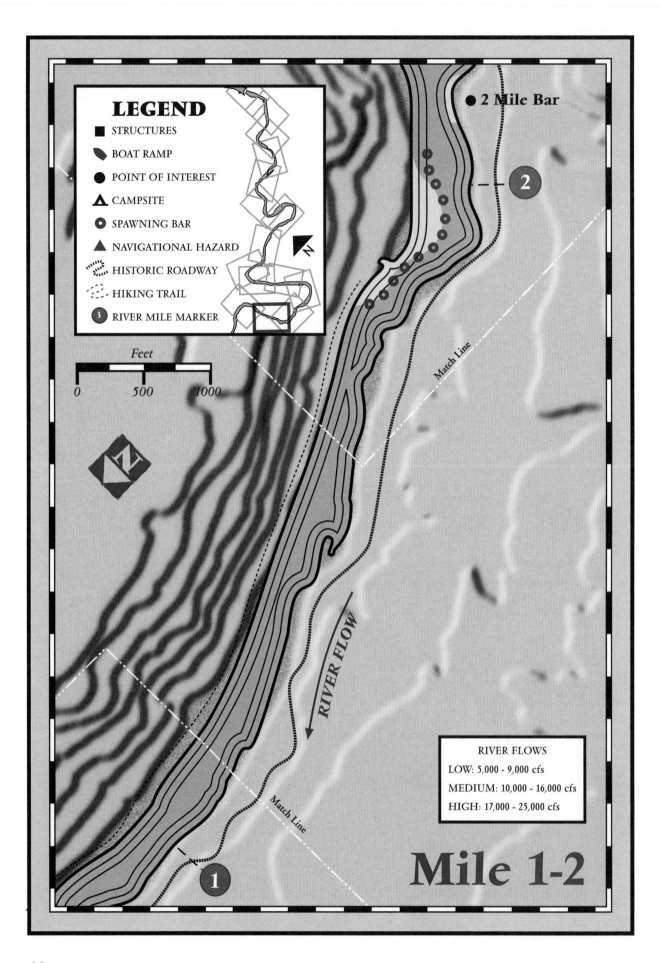

LEGEND

■ STRUCTURES

◣ BOAT RAMP

● POINT OF INTEREST

▲ CAMPSITE

⊙ SPAWNING BAR

▲ NAVIGATIONAL HAZARD

HISTORIC ROADWAY

HIKING TRAIL

③ RIVER MILE MARKER

N

Feet

0   500   1000

N

● 2 Mile Bar

2

Match Line

Match Line

RIVER FLOW

RIVER FLOWS

LOW: 5,000 - 9,000 cfs

MEDIUM: 10,000 - 16,000 cfs

HIGH: 17,000 - 25,000 cfs

1

Mile 1-2

Mile 2.0

Two Mile Bar, on the right, offers a limited fishing area. Deeply drifted nymphs are often productive in the small riffle. Try floating dry flies in the scum line that often forms here. Spin fishers should cast from the eddy out toward the edge of the current. Jigs are especially effective in this type of water. At this point on the river, the canyon walls tower about 1,500 feet above the water. At the dam, the cliffs have sloped to about 700 feet above the water. On the right at mile two the Echo Peaks rise over 2,500 feet above the river. Frederick Dellenbaugh, a member of John Wesley Powell's second expedition down the Colorado River in 1871, named the peaks. Dellenbaugh climbed to the top of the peaks and discovered remarkable echoes, later described in *The Romance of the Colorado River,*

"I took it into my head to try to shoot from there into the water of Glen Canyon beneath us and borrowed Bishop's 44-caliber Remington revolver for the purpose. When I pulled the trigger I was positively startled by the violence of the report, a deafening shock like a thousand thunder-claps in one; then dead silence. Next, from far away there was a rattle as of musketry and peal after peal of the echoing shot came back to us. The interval of silence was timed on another trial and was found to be exactly twenty seconds. The result was always the same, and from this unusual echo we named the place Echo Peaks."

After leading the second complete trip through the Grand Canyon, Robert Brewster Stanton returned to the river to operate the Hoskaninni Mining Company from 1897-1902. The company laid claim to 162 miles of river bottom, but failed when the gold proved too fine to be extracted from the river sands. Photo courtesy of Grand Canyon National Park.

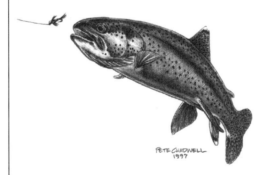

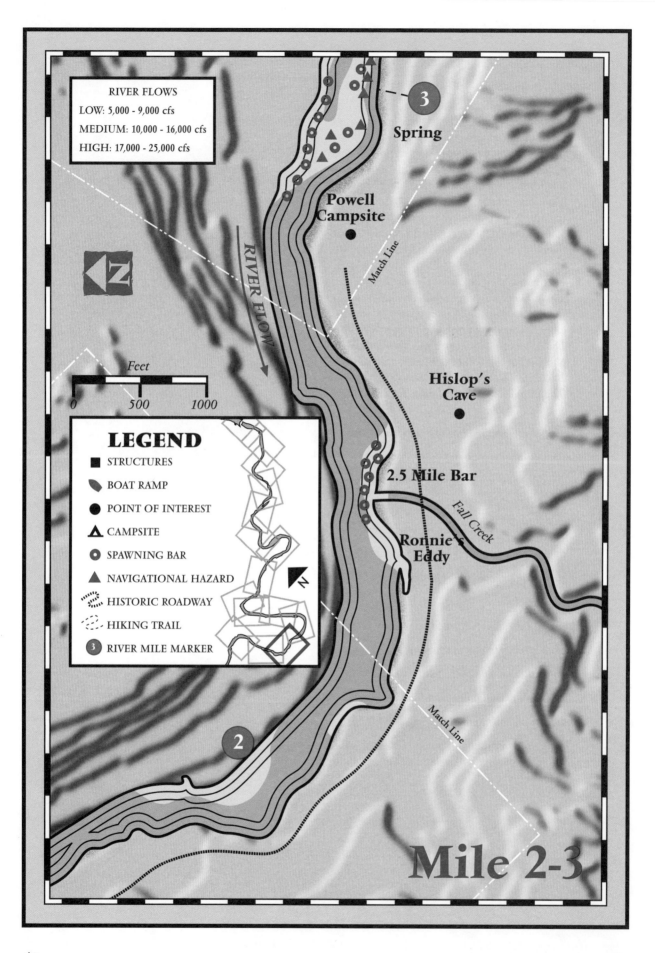

RIVER FLOWS
LOW: 5,000 - 9,000 cfs
MEDIUM: 10,000 - 16,000 cfs
HIGH: 17,000 - 25,000 cfs

3

Spring

Powell Campsite

Match Line

RIVER FLOW

Hislop's Cave

Feet

0   500   1000

LEGEND

■ STRUCTURES

◗ BOAT RAMP

● POINT OF INTEREST

▲ CAMPSITE

⊙ SPAWNING BAR

▲ NAVIGATIONAL HAZARD

HISTORIC ROADWAY

HIKING TRAIL

3 RIVER MILE MARKER

N

2.5 Mile Bar

Fall Creek

Ronnie's Eddy

Match Line

2

Mile 2-3

Mile 2.3

Two and One-Half Mile Bar. This is the first area (on the right) regularly used by fly fishers. Typically, good numbers of smaller fish inhabit the area. Extended drift tactics at the lower end are effective. Boulders at the upper end of the bar also create holding water. Use dry fly and dropper rigs. Spin fishers should cast jigs and lures in the eddy or use drift baits over the deep water bar between here and Two Mile Bar. In the spring and during summer thunderstorms, upstream winds often cause high waves in this area. Boaters should pull over and wait out these usually brief storms.

On the right, at the base of the cliff, look for Hislop's Cave, named for John Hislop, a member of the 1889-1890 Stanton expeditions. Hislop and other early visitors inscribed their names in the back of this alcove. Traveling upstream in 1900, George Wharton James wrote:

"To our right we saw an immense cave, a perfect Roman arch, covering a mouth of gigantic proportions. Some years ago a band of Navajos crossed into Utah, killed a Mr. Whitemore who owned a large band of sheep, and, it being winter and the river frozen over at Lee's Ferry, the Indians sprinkled sand upon the ice and drove the sheep into this cave for secure hiding. Since that time it has been the rendezvous of a noted band of horse thieves." (Wharton, 1942)

George James is referring to James Whitmore, killed along with his assistant in 1866 near Pipe Springs. The incident touched off the Blackhawk War.

Mile 2.5

The eddy on the left may develop a scum line. Look for surface feeding fish.

Mile 2.8

John Wesley Powell camped on the right side of the river, just upstream of the canyon that enters here. He found recent evidence of Indian occupancy including some ceramics and "an old house" made of stones, poles and grasses.

Mile 2.9

Three Mile Bar, on the left, extends to mile 3.4. At flows of 6,000 cfs and under, fly fishers can wade the bar to the left of the channel. This part of the bar is exposed at flows of 5,000 cfs or less. There is good fly fishing in the shallows on the right bank just upstream. This is one of the most popular drifts for spin fishers. Three Mile Bar poses a serious navigational hazard at flows of less than 8,000 cfs, although it is navigable along the right side at the lowest of flows.

This boiler is left over from Charles Spencer's failed gold mining operation. Photo by Dave Foster.

Surveyor John Hislop, a member of both Stanton expeditions, left this inscription at the rear of the alcove that bears his name at mile 2.3. Photo by Dave Foster.

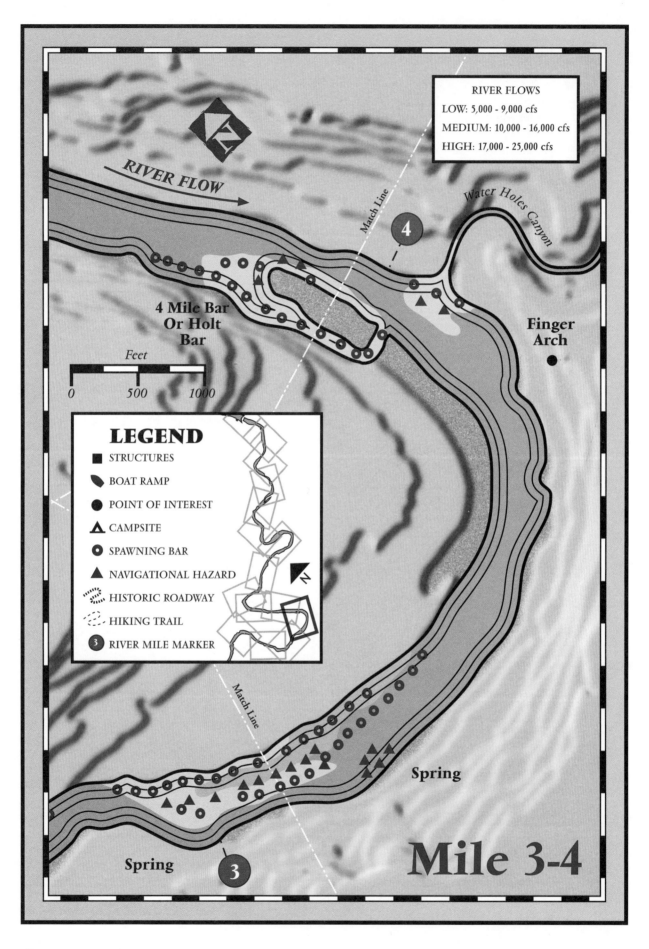

RIVER FLOW

RIVER FLOWS
LOW: 5,000 - 9,000 cfs
MEDIUM: 10,000 - 16,000 cfs
HIGH: 17,000 - 25,000 cfs

Match Line

Water Holes Canyon

4

4 Mile Bar
Or Holt
Bar

Finger
Arch

Feet

0   500   1000

LEGEND

■ STRUCTURES

◣ BOAT RAMP

● POINT OF INTEREST

△ CAMPSITE

◎ SPAWNING BAR

▲ NAVIGATIONAL HAZARD

⋰ HISTORIC ROADWAY

⋯ HIKING TRAIL

③ RIVER MILE MARKER

N

Match Line

Spring

Spring

3

Mile 3-4

42

Mile 3.7

Finger Arch is visible on the right wall.

Mile 3.9

Water Holes Canyon enters from the right. A short distance up the canyon is a dry 500 foot waterfall. A spectacular display of red bud trees blooms in this canyon in the spring. Boaters need to watch for submerged boulders at the mouth of this canyon. Drift fishing is very good from here back downstream to Three Mile Bar, especially on the inside of the bend.

Mile 4.0

Four Mile Bar, on the left side, is one of the most popular on the river and offers fly fishers opportunities at virtually all water levels. The bar is bisected on the downstream edge by a trough. DO NOT ATTEMPT TO CROSS THE TROUGH except in VERY low water. People have drowned here. Even at low flows, take great care not to become stranded by rising water.

November through March, spawning fish use this entire bar. Avoid walking on the redds. The riffle at the head of the bar and the drop off, where the trough exits the bar, hold fish throughout the entire year. Flows over 15,000 cfs cover this bar completely. As water spills over the bar, fish congregate in the shallows below. The upstream side of the trough is safely fishable to approximately 17,000 cfs. In May and June the bar is also a spawning area for Flannelmouth suckers. These fish are protected and should not be molested.

A fly fisherman at Four Mile Bar. Water Holes Canyon is in the background, upper right. Photo by Dave Foster.

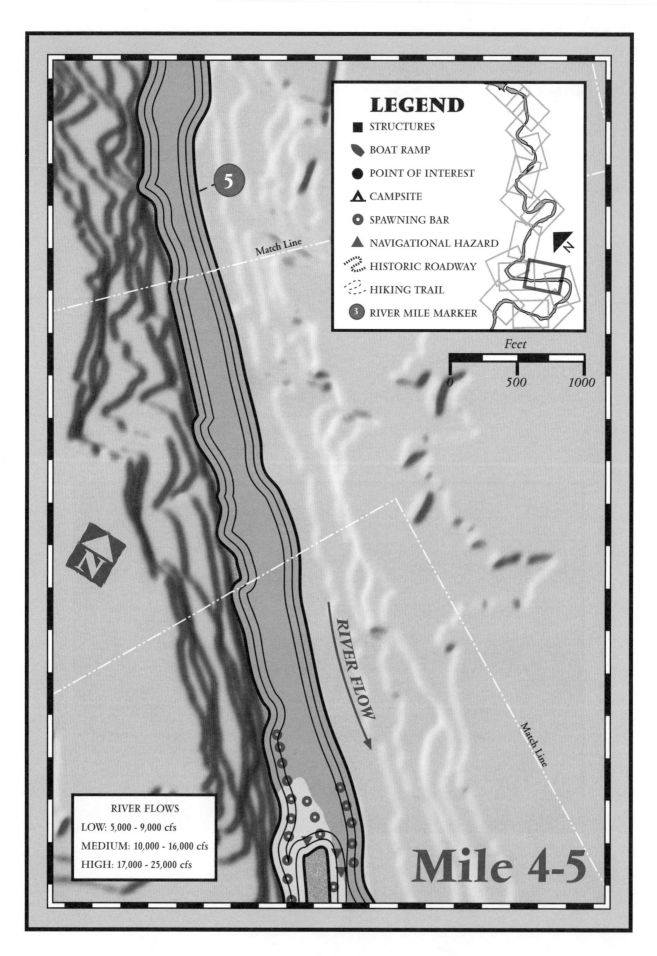

LEGEND

■ STRUCTURES

◣ BOAT RAMP

● POINT OF INTEREST

△ CAMPSITE

◉ SPAWNING BAR

▲ NAVIGATIONAL HAZARD

HISTORIC ROADWAY

HIKING TRAIL

③ RIVER MILE MARKER

Match Line

Feet

0   500   1000

RIVER FLOW

RIVER FLOWS
LOW: 5,000 - 9,000 cfs

MEDIUM: 10,000 - 16,000 cfs

HIGH: 17,000 - 25,000 cfs

Mile 4-5

Mile 4.0

The small eddy on the right develops a good scum line at medium to high flows.

Mile 4.0 to 5.0

An excellent spin fishing stretch extends from Four Mile Bar upstream to mile 5.0. Drift fishing, casting lures and jigs are all effective here. Avoid drifting through fly fishers on the upstream tip of Four Mile Bar.

Fly fishing the top of Four Mile Bar. Photo by Dave Foster.

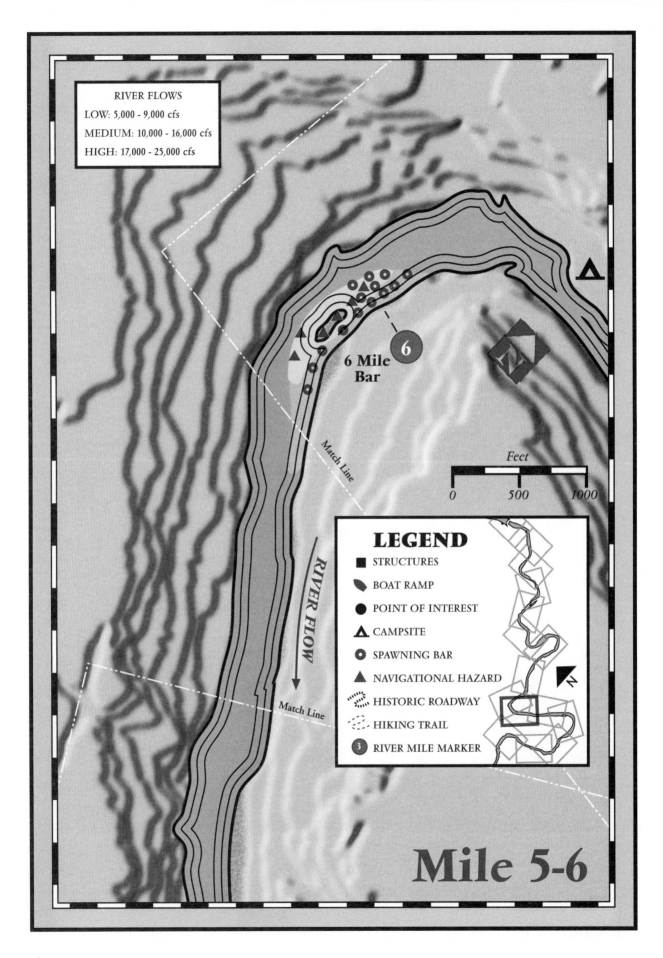

RIVER FLOWS
LOW: 5,000 - 9,000 cfs
MEDIUM: 10,000 - 16,000 cfs
HIGH: 17,000 - 25,000 cfs

6 Mile Bar

6

Match Line

RIVER FLOW

Match Line

Feet

0   500   1000

LEGEND

■ STRUCTURES

◣ BOAT RAMP

● POINT OF INTEREST

▲ CAMPSITE

◎ SPAWNING BAR

▲ NAVIGATIONAL HAZARD

⁘ HISTORIC ROADWAY

⋯ HIKING TRAIL

③ RIVER MILE MARKER

N

Mile 5-6

Mile 5.7

Six Mile Bar is located to the right of mid-channel. Flows of approximately 9,000 cfs just cover this bar, creating a serious boating hazard. The channel is to the left side of the river. This bar is best fly fished at lower flows to about 10,000 cfs. At higher flows, the bar loses definition and holding water. It is un-fishable with flows over 12,000 cfs. The slow water in front is productive spin fishing water.

Mile 5.8

The eddy on the left develops a good scum line and often holds fish dining on midges. It can also be effectively fished with light jigs or lures. Be prepared for subtle takes on the sink when fishing jigs.

Lunch on the boat. Photo by Dave Foster.

Native Fishes

Prior to the completion of the dam, the free-flowing river was home to eight native fish species. Five are endemic, meaning they occur nowhere else. Most of these fish are now endangered or extinct due to the lowered water temperature and competition with non-native species. The species include the razorback sucker, Colorado River squawfish, flannelmouth sucker, bluehead sucker, humpback chub, bonytail chub, roundtail chub, and speckled dace. Of these fish, the bluehead sucker and flannelmouth sucker are most likely to be encountered in the Lee's Ferry reach of the Colorado River. This is especially true at the mouth of the Paria River and at Four Mile Bar which are spawning areas for both flannelmouth and bluehead suckers in the late spring and early summer. If you catch these or any other native fish you should immediately return them, unharmed, to the river.

Native fishes of the Colorado River.
Clockwise from upper left: Bluehead sucker, bonytail chub, humpback chub, and flannelmouth sucker. Photo courtesy of United States Department of Agriculture.

The Colorado River pike minnow is considered extirpated from the river below Glen Canyon Dam. The pike minnow is the largest member of the minnow family. The largest specimen on record from the Colorado River weighed about 110 pounds. Photo courtesy of United States Department of Agriculture.

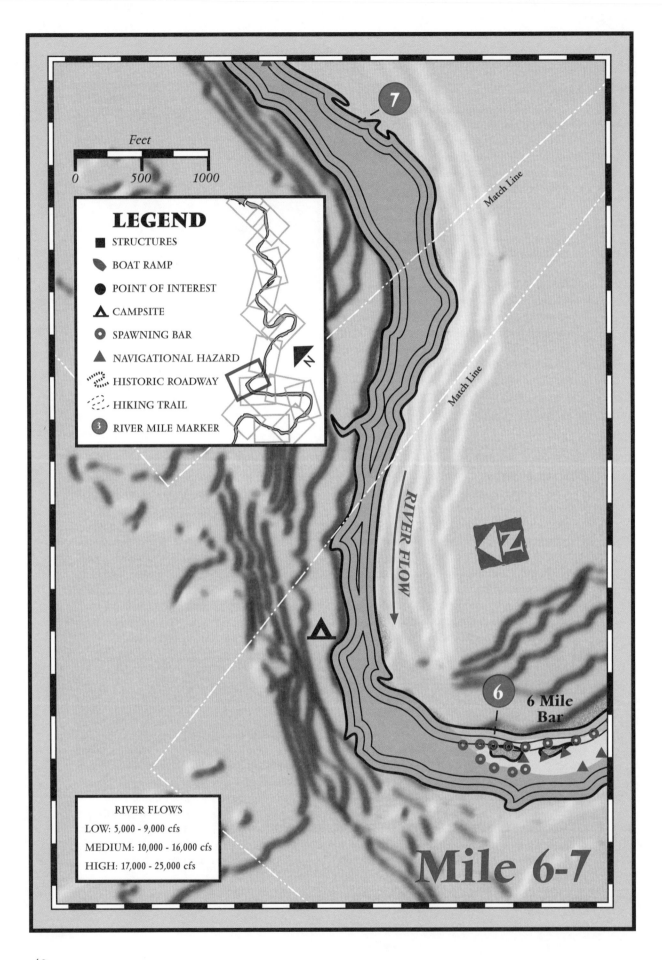

LEGEND

■ STRUCTURES

⬟ BOAT RAMP

● POINT OF INTEREST

▲ CAMPSITE

◉ SPAWNING BAR

▲ NAVIGATIONAL HAZARD

⋯ HISTORIC ROADWAY

⋯ HIKING TRAIL

3 RIVER MILE MARKER

Feet

0   500   1000

Match Line

Match Line

RIVER FLOW

7

6

6 Mile
Bar

RIVER FLOWS

LOW: 5,000 - 9,000 cfs

MEDIUM: 10,000 - 16,000 cfs

HIGH: 17,000 - 25,000 cfs

Mile 6-7

Mile 6.2

Six Mile Campground, on the left. Beware: fluctuating water can strand boats in the boulders here.

Mile 6.6

Jig fishing is good from the rocky point on the left downstream to mile 6.3.

Mile 6.7

Spectacular crossbeds on both walls. A grand waterfall comes off the left wall during heavy summer rains. Just seeing this fall is worth the trip upriver.

Beaver are common along the Colorado River between Lees Ferry and Glen Canyon Dam, although rarely seen due to their nocturnal nature. Their dens are built in riverbanks, and their tracks and trails are often seen on sandy beaches. Photo by Dave Foster.

The Old High Water Mark

Before Glen Canyon Dam, the near-river vegetation was subjected to the ravages of a raging, runoff-swollen Colorado River. Limited streamside vegetation included short-lived grasses or the occasional woody plant or shrub that happened to germinate in an area protected from the annual floods. This scour zone extended up canyon walls to approximately the 100,000 cfs mark. At or just above the 100,000 cfs water line, high enough to escape the annual flood waters, is the old high water vegetation zone. In Glen and upper Marble Canyons, this zone has redbud, netleaf hackberry, apache plume and scrub oak. In certain areas, such as Three Mile Bar (on the right) this vegetation line is still visible 20-30 feet above current average high flows.

What Are Those Trees?

Today's dominant streamside vegetation is tamarisk or salt cedar. This phreatophyte (plant roots reach the water table) was introduced to the United States from the Mediterranean before 1900. Unparalleled in its ability to invade beaches and producing huge numbers of wind borne seeds, tamarisk established itself throughout the Colorado River drainage by the 1930's. Other exotics have invaded this portion of the Colorado including elm and Russian olive.

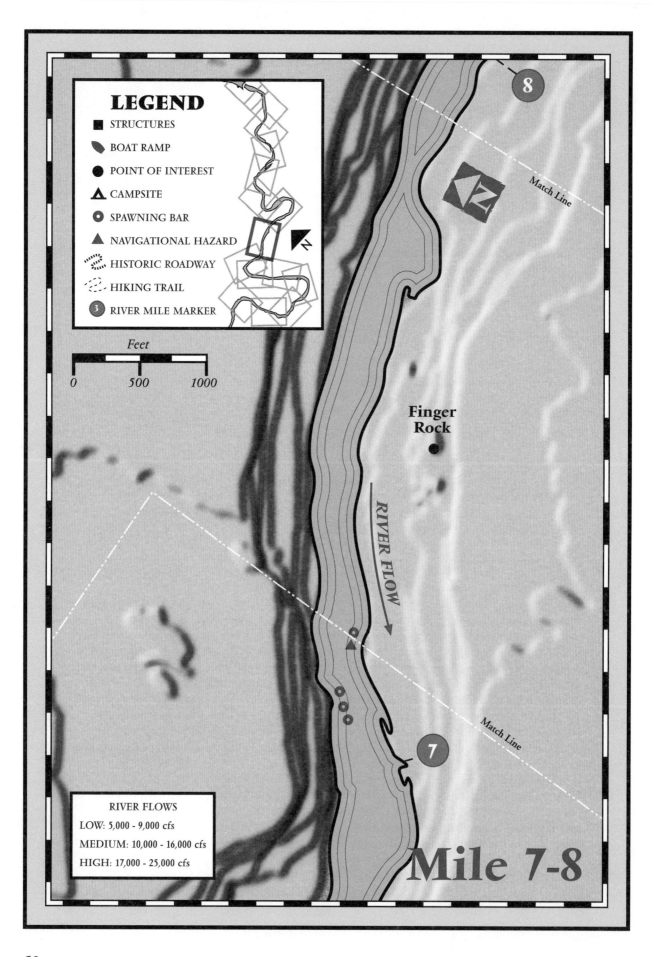

LEGEND

- ■ STRUCTURES
- 🔲 BOAT RAMP
- ● POINT OF INTEREST
- △ CAMPSITE
- ◎ SPAWNING BAR
- ▲ NAVIGATIONAL HAZARD
- ⋮⋮ HISTORIC ROADWAY
- ⋰ HIKING TRAIL
- ③ RIVER MILE MARKER

N

Feet

0   500   1000

8

Match Line

Finger
Rock

RIVER FLOW

7

Match Line

RIVER FLOWS

LOW: 5,000 - 9,000 cfs

MEDIUM: 10,000 - 16,000 cfs

HIGH: 17,000 - 25,000 cfs

Mile 7-8

Mile 7.2

There is a large boulder on the right side of the channel. It is a boating hazard at flows less than 7,000 cfs.

Mile 7.3

Finger Rock is on the right side.

Mile 7.9

Fish frequently feed in the dense scum line that forms in the eddy on the left side. Seven and a Half Mile Bar is on the right and is a good fly fishing bar at all flows. The riffle at the top of the bar is productive, especially late spring through fall. There is some spawning gravel above this riffle, with fish moving to it November through March. Water covers these beds at about 6,000 cfs and fishing is good up to about 12,000 cfs. Year-round the eddy at the bottom of the bar generally holds midging fish. Woolly Buggers are also effective. At extremely high flows, fish cruise along the weeds in front of the campground searching for terrestrials.

"On the walls, and back many miles into the country, numerous monument shaped buttes are observed. So we have a curious ensemble of wonderful features - carved walls, royal arches, glens, gulches, mounds and monuments. From which of these features shall we select a name? We decided to call it Glen Canyon." From John Wesley Powell's "The Exploration of the Colorado River and Its Canyons" August 3, 1869. Powell was leader of the first trip through the canyons of the Green and Colorado Rivers. Photo by Dave Foster.

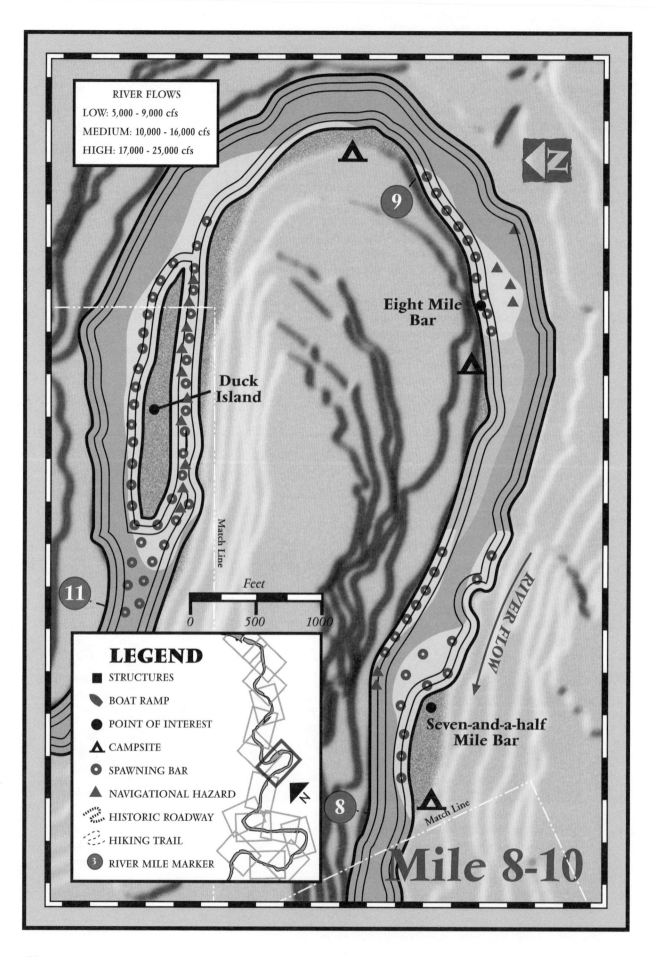

RIVER FLOWS
LOW: 5,000 - 9,000 cfs
MEDIUM: 10,000 - 16,000 cfs
HIGH: 17,000 - 25,000 cfs

9

Eight Mile
Bar

Duck
Island

Match Line

11

Feet

0   500   1000

Seven-and-a-half
Mile Bar

8

Match Line

LEGEND

■ STRUCTURES

◗ BOAT RAMP

● POINT OF INTEREST

▲ CAMPSITE

◎ SPAWNING BAR

▲ NAVIGATIONAL HAZARD

⠿ HISTORIC ROADWAY

⠂ HIKING TRAIL

③ RIVER MILE MARKER

N

RIVER FLOW

Mile 8-10

Mile 8.1

The bar on the left, directly across the river from Seven and a Half Mile Bar, is an excellent low-water fly fishing area, at flows of less than 8,000 cfs. This water is fast and deep even at low flows, requiring extra leader and weight. Make very steep, upstream casts along the bank. Just above the deep water run is a gravel bar that holds fish year-round. In spring and summer, fish dry flies during rising water. In winter, spawning fish gather here on small patches of gravel.

Mile 8.3

This short run on the right bank often holds numerous fish only accessible to fly fishers at flows of 8,000 cfs or less. For spin fishers, the area from mile 7.9 to mile 9.0 is productive at all water levels.

Mile 8.5

Eight Mile Bar and campground are on the left. A very popular and productive bar extends from mile 8.5 to mile 8.75, and typically holds fish all year. During November - March spawning, fish generally concentrate in the clean gravel areas. The remainder of the year they are distributed the entire length of the bar. Midge hatches can be very prolific. With the shallow water and slower current in the lower part of the bar, fish often rise to dry flies, including tiny dry midge imitations. During summer, fish often hold and cruise the sandy flats in the lower bar. Try a variety of dry flies. Study this bar carefully, fish are often much closer than you think. A common mistake is to wade in too deep, which drives fish out of the shallows. There is no sun here November through early March.

Mile 8.8

This stretch is extremely hazardous to navigate at flows less than 8,000 cfs. Boaters, note the bar in the center of the channel that extends out at the top of Eight Mile Bar. Bear to the right of the channel. There is a well-developed back eddy on the right just above the bar. A huge boulder sits in the middle of the eddy. This spot usually holds fish midging in a scum line.

Mile 9.0

Nine Mile Campground is on the left. The shallow, extended beach here is notorious for stranding boats during widely fluctuating flows. Anchor your boat offshore.

Mile 9.1

Nine Mile Bar, on the left, is one of the largest on the river. The best anchoring area is at the bottom of the bar, in the eddy in front of the campsite. The entire bar is fishable more than a quarter-mile upstream. Look for subtle seams along this bar, where most fish hold. Dry fly and dropper tactics are effective in the very slow water at the top. The upper bar gets sun in the winter. Spin fishers work this drift all the way to the top of Duck Island. About two-thirds up the bar, some ten feet up the cliff face, Isaac Carling Spencer left an inscription. Spencer moved to Lee's Ferry in 1925 at the request of his brother-in-law Jeremiah Johnson. Johnson lived at Lee's Ferry off and on from 1875-1949.

Mile 9.4

Duck Island, on the left. Boaters want to stay in the channel to the right of the island. This is one of the most popular fly fishing areas on the river. The riffle on the top of the bar holds many fish and is best at medium to low flows when the riffle is highly defined. This is a very straightforward and easy riffle to fish. The backside of the bar also fishes best at medium to low flows. The top of the inside is an excellent area. Fishing becomes more challenging downstream into the slower water. During the November - March spawning season, fish nest around the entire island. A freshwater limestone bed (deposited millions of years ago in a recurring lake or playa) is visible in the left wall near Duck Island.

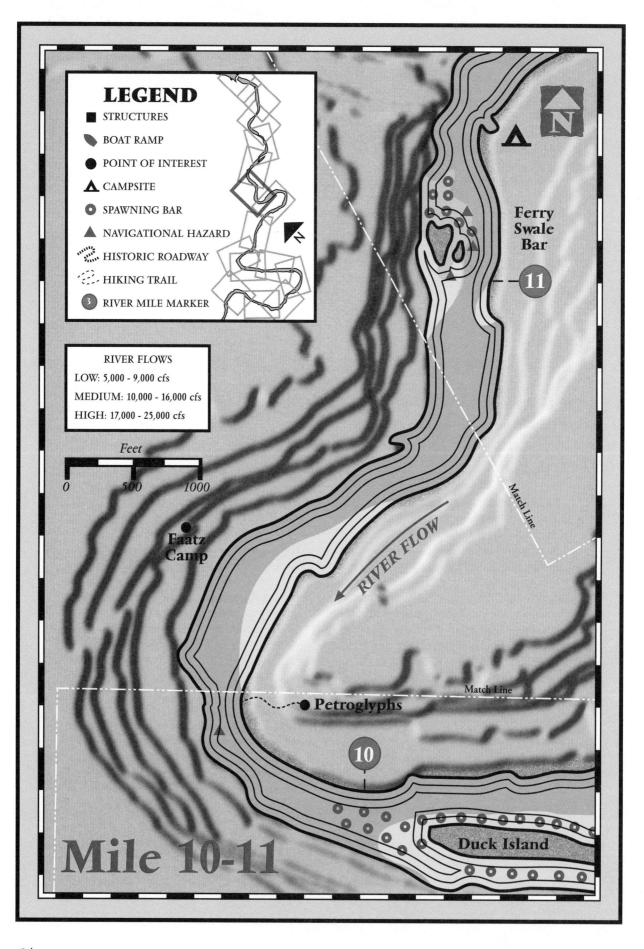

LEGEND

- ■ STRUCTURES
- BOAT RAMP
- ● POINT OF INTEREST
- △ CAMPSITE
- ◉ SPAWNING BAR
- ▲ NAVIGATIONAL HAZARD
- HISTORIC ROADWAY
- HIKING TRAIL
- ③ RIVER MILE MARKER

RIVER FLOWS
LOW: 5,000 - 9,000 cfs

MEDIUM: 10,000 - 16,000 cfs

HIGH: 17,000 - 25,000 cfs

Feet

0   500   1000

Faatz
Camp

RIVER FLOW

Match Line

Match Line

Ferry
Swale
Bar

⑪

Petroglyphs

⑩

Duck Island

Mile 10-11

Mile 0

A wakeless zone extends from the dock to the upstream buoys. Boaters are prohibited below the downstream cable. A bed of Shinarump conglomerate juts steeply from the river opposite the boat ramp and slightly downstream. This is Lee's Backbone. From 1873 to 1898, a road atop it provided access from the south to the upper ferry site. The Dugway road, finished in 1898, parallels the river on the cliff face opposite the mouth of the Paria River. This road allowed travelers to trade a toilsome trip over "the Backbone" for a precipitous trip over the one-lane road a hundred feet above the river.

Mile .4

The wreckage of the Charles H. Spencer is on the left bank. In 1911, the steamboat was shipped from San Francisco in several pieces. It was to carry coal from Warm Creek (28 miles upstream) to a gold mining operation at Lee's Ferry. It cost $30,000, was 87 feet long, and was named for the engineer in charge of American Placer Corporation's operation at Lee's Ferry.

Mile .6

Look for cables from the ferry on the right bank, and a road leading to the ferry landing. Track cables were installed in 1896 while James Emett was ferry operator. Before this time, the ferry master simply rowed passengers across the river. An inscription, "SELMA 1923," is visible on a large boulder just below the ferry site and approximately fifty feet above river level. Many other inscriptions are nearby. On the left bank note the ruins of a way station used by early ferry travelers.

Mile .65

Hunting and loaded firearms are not permitted from this point downstream.

Mile .8

On the right, for approximately one and a half miles, is a road built in 1899 by mining engineer Robert Brewster Stanton. Stanton is best known as the leader of the second group to complete a river trip through Grand Canyon. He returned to Glen Canyon to operate the Hoskaninni Mining Company from 1897-1902. The company laid claim to 162 miles of Glen Canyon and intended to dredge the entire river bottom. To this end they brought in a 105 foot long floating dredge. Stanton's road was built as assessment work was required to keep the mining claims valid.

Mile 2.0

Two Mile Bar, on the right, offers a limited fishing area. Deeply drifted nymphs are often productive in the small riffle. Try floating dry flies in the scum line that often forms here. Spin fishers should cast from the eddy out toward the edge of the current. Jigs are especially effective in this type of water. At this point on the river, the canyon walls tower about 1,500 feet above the water. At the dam, the cliffs have sloped to about 700

Anasazi presence in Glen Canyon is evidenced by Glen Canyon Style Four petroglyphs near mile 10, right side.

Inscription at mile 10.4, left side.

A culture far older than the Anasazi created the square-bodied anthropomorphs and animal figures known as Glen Canyon Style Five petroglyphs. It is generally agreed that this type of rock art is 4,000 years old. Photos on this page by Dave Foster.

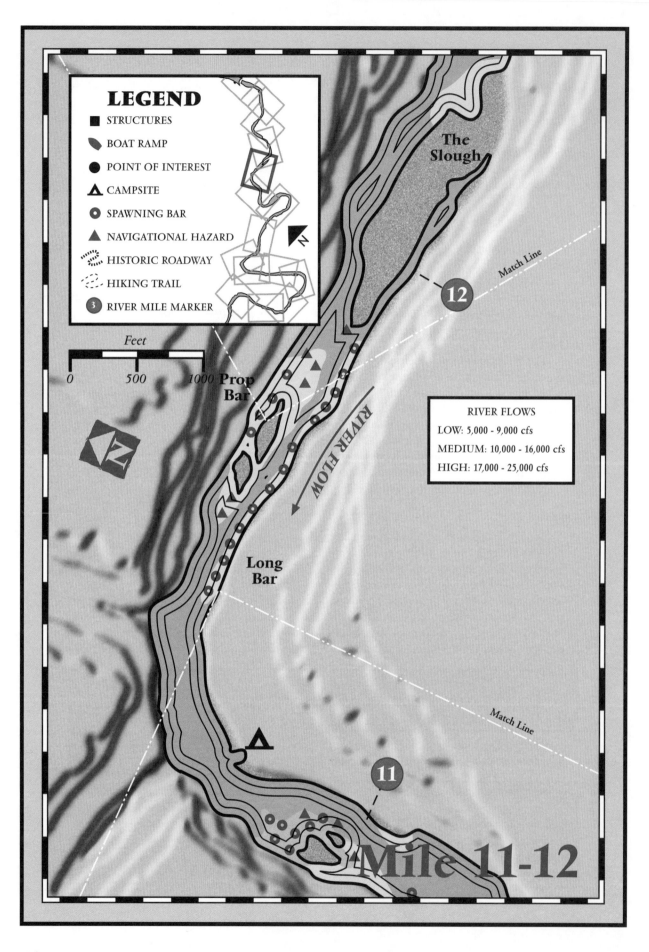

LEGEND

■ STRUCTURES

▬ BOAT RAMP

● POINT OF INTEREST

▲ CAMPSITE

◉ SPAWNING BAR

▲ NAVIGATIONAL HAZARD

HISTORIC ROADWAY

HIKING TRAIL

③ RIVER MILE MARKER

N

The Slough

Match Line

12

Feet

0   500   1000   Prop Bar

RIVER FLOW

N

RIVER FLOWS
LOW: 5,000 - 9,000 cfs
MEDIUM: 10,000 - 16,000 cfs
HIGH: 17,000 - 25,000 cfs

Long Bar

Match Line

▲

11

Mile 11-12

Mile 11.0

Ferry Swale Bar is mid-channel and extends to the left bank, posing a hazard to boaters. Take the channel along the right bank. An excellent fly fishing bar at low to medium flows, wading Ferry Swale Bar becomes difficult at flows greater than 15,000 cfs. At approximately 5,000 cfs, a channel forms, bisecting the island. As the water continues to rise and washes food from the bar, trout will often feed vigorously at the downstream end of this channel. In winter, the fish move to the smaller gravel on the upstream side of the bar to spawn. On the right bank, find a good dry fly eddy just slightly below Ferry Swale Bar. Approach it slowly to spot fish sipping midges from the surface.

Mile 11.1

Ferry Swale Camp is on the right. This large camp is one of the most popular on the river. Spin fishers often find good fishing from this point downstream to mile 10.5. The three eddies on the left bank from this point to mile 11.5 often hold surface feeding fish. Try midge imitations as well as attractors such as Humpies and Renegades.

Sunny day, tight line. Photo by Dave Foster.

Mile 11.4

Long Bar, on the right, extends to mile 11.7. This relatively deep, fast run can be a challenge, but is known for large, robust fish. You can usually see fish holding close to the bank. The best technique is to float a long, drag-free drift downstream. Sometimes "walking the dog" is effective. The current is fast here and many good fish break off. Be sure to strike downstream to get a good hook set and move downstream to stay parallel with a running fish. A well-developed eddy on the left, at the dry waterfall, often holds fish eating midges. Fish from an anchored boat.

Mile 11.7

Prop Bar, on the left, is aptly named and poses a hazard at all levels. Heading upstream in the early morning, glare often makes it impossible to see. Heading downstream the bar rises gradually, giving no clue of its presence until it is too late. Be alert and stay to the right of the channel, heading upstream. This is one of the most popular fly fishing spots on the river. It's a large area and can accommodate many anglers, so don't expect to be alone. At low flows, fish tend to congregate in the riffles at the top and bottom. Fish are also scattered throughout the front of the bar between these two points. This bar really turns on with rising water. At between 8,000-9,000 cfs water begins to flow in the channel that bisects the bar. Fish congregate where this channel exits into the main river and feed vigorously in the riffle at the top of the channel as water begins to flow through. As water rises, fish also congregate and begin feeding along the drop off below the lower bar. Approximately 15,000 cfs will cover the entire bar and at this flow fish begin to disperse. Wading becomes hazardous at about 16,000 cfs.

Mile 11.8

The channel narrows at this point between the upstream tip of Prop Bar and the downstream tip of Twelve Mile Bar. Navigate very carefully.

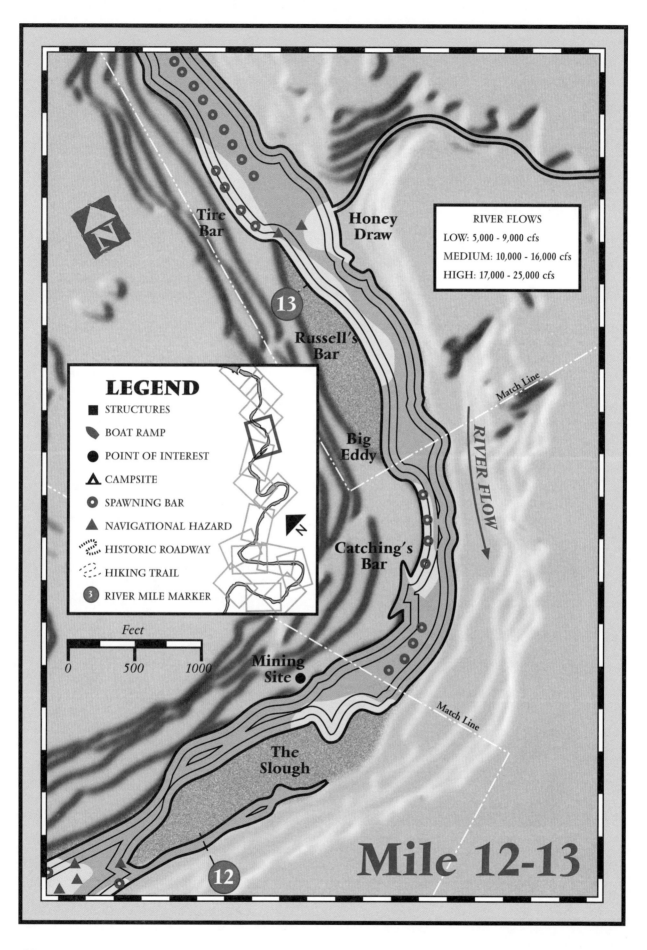

Tire Bar

Honey Draw

RIVER FLOWS
LOW: 5,000 - 9,000 cfs
MEDIUM: 10,000 - 16,000 cfs
HIGH: 17,000 - 25,000 cfs

13

Russell's Bar

Match Line

RIVER FLOW

Big Eddy

LEGEND

■ STRUCTURES
◣ BOAT RAMP
● POINT OF INTEREST
▲ CAMPSITE
◉ SPAWNING BAR
▲ NAVIGATIONAL HAZARD
▨ HISTORIC ROADWAY
⬚ HIKING TRAIL
③ RIVER MILE MARKER

N

Catching's Bar

Feet

0   500   1000

Mining Site ●

Match Line

The Slough

12

Mile 12-13

58

Mile 12.0

Twelve Mile Bar or "The Slough". Fly fishers will need long leaders (12 feet plus) and lots of weight when fishing this very deep run along the right bank. The riffle at the top of the bar is also good. The long slough behind the back of the bar holds good numbers of carp, especially in low, warm water. These fish can be extremely spooky and difficult to take on a fly and offer an interesting and humbling change from casting to trout.

Mile 12.2

On the left-hand cliff approximately 15 feet above the river are carved steps, probably made during a gold prospecting operation in the gravel on the bench above. The site dates to a little known depression-era gold mining period in Glen Canyon.

Mile 12.4

Catching's Eddy. A favorite drift for spin fishers, on the left, extends from this point downstream to mile 12.2.

Mile 12.5

Catching's Bar. A mid-channel bar poses a navigational hazard at flows of 5,500 cfs or less. This bar seems to fish best during extreme low or high flows, below 8,000 cfs or above 20,000 cfs. High flows during the spawning season give fish access to the gravel along the upper end of the bar. The eddy below the bar sometimes holds midging fish.

Mile 12.6

Big Eddy is on the left and fishes well for spin fishers using jigs. This is a great place to anchor and cast on a windy day.

Mile 12.7

Thirteen Mile Bar or Russell's Bar, on the left, is another very popular bar offering varied fishing. The eddy at the bottom often holds cruising fish that will take a dry. Above this, a series of seams hold fish. Look for midging fish in the small eddies associated with these seams. The riffle at the top fishes well during rising water, as invertebrates are washed off the gravel bar above. This is one of the bars that fishes well even during very high flows of over 20,000 cfs. Fish move into the long, broad riffle that forms almost the entire length of the bar.

Anglers moving into position at mile 12. Photo by Dave Foster.

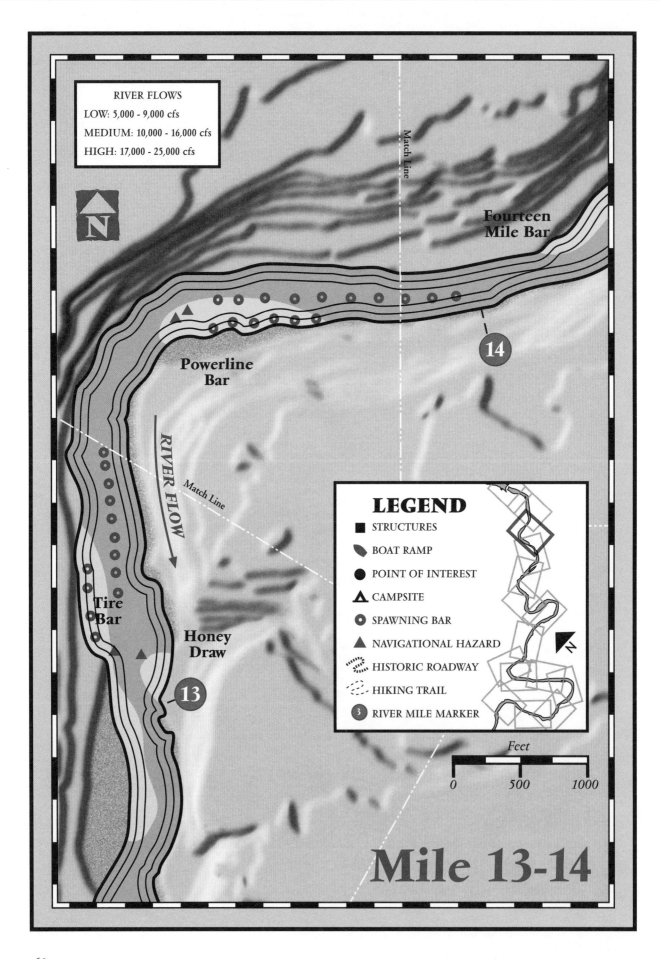

RIVER FLOWS
LOW: 5,000 - 9,000 cfs
MEDIUM: 10,000 - 16,000 cfs
HIGH: 17,000 - 25,000 cfs

N

Match Line

Fourteen
Mile Bar

Powerline
Bar

14

RIVER FLOW

Match Line

Tire
Bar

Honey
Draw

13

LEGEND

■ STRUCTURES

◤ BOAT RAMP

● POINT OF INTEREST

▲ CAMPSITE

◉ SPAWNING BAR

▲ NAVIGATIONAL HAZARD

⌇ HISTORIC ROADWAY

⌇ HIKING TRAIL

3 RIVER MILE MARKER

N

Feet

0   500   1000

Mile 13-14

Mile 13.0

Honey Draw, on the right side, has a narrow, boulder-filled channel at the mouth that requires cautious boating at all flows. It is most hazardous at flows of 8,000 cfs or less. The riffle here is a good nymphing area with scuds and other standard Lee's Ferry nymphs when flows are less than 10,000 cfs. A popular spin fishing drift extends upstream to the spring leaping from the right hand wall at mile 13.3. You will find a small, cool fern garden and seep in the cleft here.

Mile 13.1

Tire Bar, on the left, is named for the large tractor tire at the top of the bar. Fish hold out in front of this bar and along the seam at the lower end. The back side is an important spawning area that becomes fishable at flows of 10,000 cfs. Avoid walking through the spawning gravel November through March.

Mile 13.5

Powerline Bar, on the right, always holds fish. Spring, summer and fall find fish congregating in the riffle at the lower end of the bar. Spawning gravel attracts fish to the upper part of the bar November to March. These fish hold very tight to the bank and are difficult to see due to the glare off the left wall. Cloudy conditions reduce this glare and allow sight fishing. The lower part of this bar is a good fishing location because it is protected from wind.

Mile 13.5

A good spin fishing drift extends upriver to mile 14.1. This area can also be fly fished from a drifting boat. Use extra long leaders (to twelve feet) and extra split shot.

Toasting a lovely day in a beautiful place. Photo by Dave Foster.

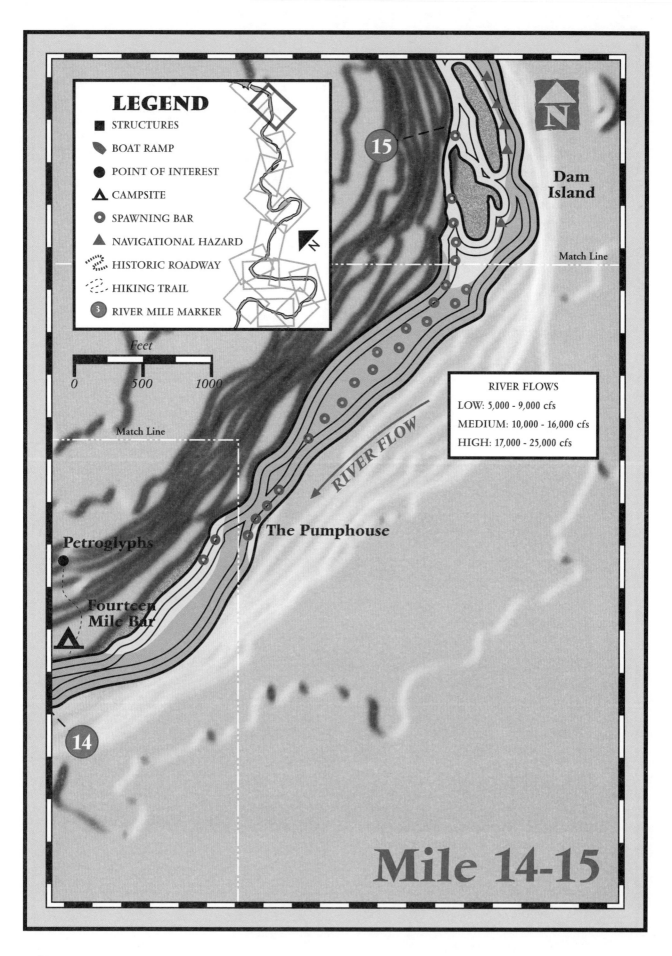

LEGEND

◼ STRUCTURES

⬩ BOAT RAMP

● POINT OF INTEREST

△ CAMPSITE

◎ SPAWNING BAR

▲ NAVIGATIONAL HAZARD

⋯ HISTORIC ROADWAY

⋯ HIKING TRAIL

③ RIVER MILE MARKER

N

15

Dam Island

Match Line

Match Line

Feet

0   500   1000

RIVER FLOWS

LOW: 5,000 - 9,000 cfs

MEDIUM: 10,000 - 16,000 cfs

HIGH: 17,000 - 25,000 cfs

RIVER FLOW

The Pumphouse

Petroglyphs

Fourteen
Mile Bar

14

Mile 14-15

Mile 14.1

Fourteen Mile Campsite is high above the river on the left. There is a hiking route from the campsite to the canyon rim and a wonderful petroglyph panel on the canyon wall behind the outhouse.

Mile 14.2

Fourteen Mile Bar, on the left, is best fished in the spring, summer and fall. It receives no sun from the first part of November through March. Good midge hatches occur here in the spring and summer months. At low and medium flows, fish the riffle at the top of the bar and along the seam at the bottom. At high flows, fish hold in the shallow riffle that forms the entire length of the bar. Spot your quarry before blindly stomping into the river, especially at the lower part of the bar where fish tend to hold close to the bank. Because of the shallow and slower water, these fish will sometimes take a tiny dry midge or midge emerger pattern at or near the surface.

Mile 14.3

The Pumphouse, on the right, fishes best during the winter spawning season. Fish often line up along the bank above the small riffle and are impossible to see in the glare. It is a challenge to get a fly to these fish without spooking them or hanging up in the trees. Roll cast from a position above the fish, and present the fly on an extended downstream drift.

Upstream to Dam Island is a great spin fishing drift. Excavation adits are visible high on the right wall. A tunnel dug from above Powerline Bar at mile 13.3 to the base of the dam allowed workmen to get to the dam site during construction. While digging this tunnel, the adits allowed material to be dumped into the canyon instead of being hauled all the way to the top.

Mile 14.8

Dam Island, on the left, is the last bar regularly fished on this stretch of river. The front side of the island offers fly fishers good nymphing water. The drop-off at the bottom of the island is especially productive during flows of 12,000 cfs and less. Use an extended drift over this drop-off to reach the deep-holding fish here. A channel at the top of the island is fishable at about 9,000 cfs. This area fishes especially well just as the water begins to flow through. At flows of over 16,000 cfs, the water around the back of the island allows fish to spawn in the gravel at the top of the channel.

All dogs should be so lucky to boat Lee's Ferry. Photo by Dave Foster.

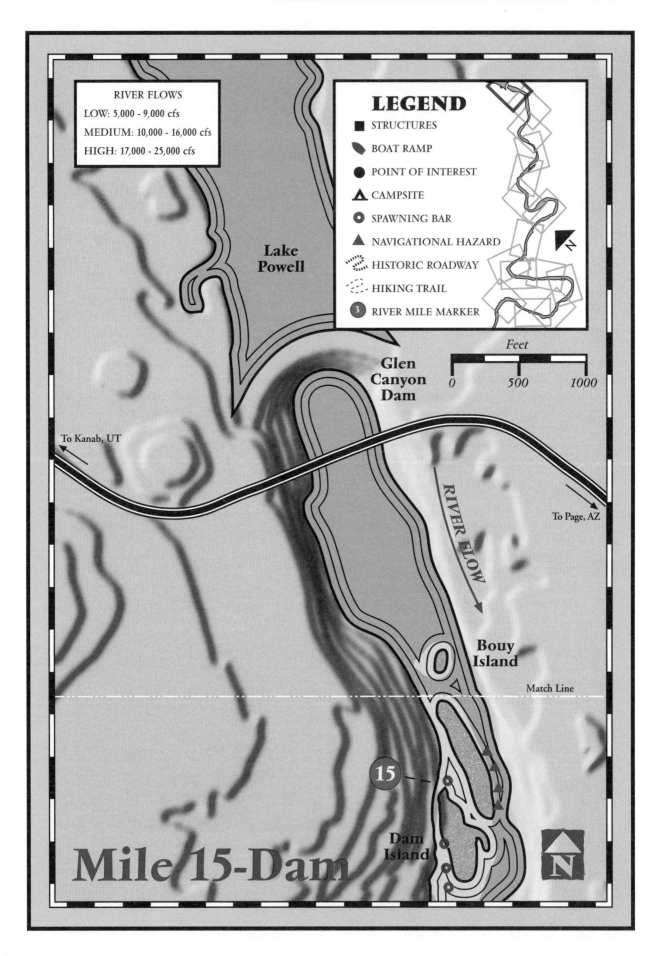

RIVER FLOWS
LOW: 5,000 - 9,000 cfs
MEDIUM: 10,000 - 16,000 cfs
HIGH: 17,000 - 25,000 cfs

LEGEND

■ STRUCTURES

🛶 BOAT RAMP

● POINT OF INTEREST

△ CAMPSITE

◉ SPAWNING BAR

▲ NAVIGATIONAL HAZARD

HISTORIC ROADWAY

HIKING TRAIL

③ RIVER MILE MARKER

Lake Powell

Glen Canyon Dam

Feet

0   500   1000

To Kanab, UT

RIVER FLOW

To Page, AZ

Bouy Island

Match Line

15

Dam Island

Mile 15-Dam

N

Mile 15.0

The rock bar on the left, above Dam Island, is made up of very irregular and slippery rocks and is extremely hazardous to wade. Very deep, swift water flows directly adjacent to the bar where at least one near drowning has occurred. Use extreme caution. Do not wade here in flows over 13,000 cfs. The Duck Pond is the slow water behind this bar. Wading is over very slippery and irregular substrate here, too. The best access to this challenging slow water is walking up along the left bank above Dam Island. Work with a spotter perched high on the left bank to help find fish and then direct your casts. Flows over 17,000 cfs cover this bar enough for productive drift fishing from a boat.

Buoy Island is wadeable to about 12,000 cfs. Fish congregate in the riffles on either side of the bar. Because of the proximity of the dam, use extreme caution in this area. Unexpected increased releases can, and do, occur without warning.

Happy angler fishing Dam Island just below Glen Canyon dam. Photo by Dave Foster.

From Dam Island, looking across the Duck Pond at Glen Canyon dam and bridge. Photo by Dave Foster.

Charles Spencer's mining operation near Lee's Ferry, circa 1912. Photo courtesty of Arizona Historical Society.

Lee's Ferry History

John Doyle Lee and wives Rachel Andora Woolsey Lee (standing) and Caroline Williams Lee. Rachel lived at Jacob's Pools, approximately twenty-five miles southwest of Lee's Ferry, where Lee had another Ranch. Arizona Historical Society photo.

Lee's Ferry History

It is obvious that the topography of the Lee's Ferry canyon country created substantial challenges for early travelers, with the Colorado River posing the greatest obstacle. The secluded Lee's Ferry site, at the mouth of the Paria River, was the last place travelers could access and cross the river above Grand Canyon. The river then becomes entirely canyon bound for 280 miles downstream of the Ferry. As such, Lee's Ferry was a vital north-south passage and the region's essential travel link from the early 1860's until the Navajo Bridge was completed in 1929.

First Visitors

Recorded history of the area starts October 26, 1776. Francisco Atanasio Dominguez and Silvestre Velez de Escalante arrived leading a ragged, disheartened expedition seeking a trade route from Santa Fe, New Mexico to Monterey, California. On the trail since late July, the expedition was caught in early snowstorms near present-day Cedar City, Utah where they called it quits and began heading home. They were desperate to ford El Rio Grande de Los Cosninos, as they called the Colorado. Local Indians vaguely steered the party toward a possible river crossing in the area, but it became apparent the river was too deep and swift to be forded. For six days, the party attempted to cross on rafts and sent swimmers across to explore the route to the south to look for another possible way out of the canyon. Exploring up the Paria River (about two and half miles) a route to the canyon rim was discovered that allowed access to a crossing, later called Ute Ford and the Crossing of the Fathers. This ford was about thirty-five miles upstream of what would become Lee's Ferry. The party finally reached home in January, 1777.

The Early Days of Lee's Ferry

Eighty-two years later, on November 3, 1858, a regular crossing at the head of Grand Canyon was conceived when Mormon pioneer Jacob Hamblin viewed the area from the pass used by Escalante and Dominguez. On this, the first of a dozen expeditions Hamblin led to the Hopi villages, the explorer realized the benefits of a river crossing. In his report to Church leader Brigham Young Hamblin wrote,

"We can shorten the journey four or five days and shun the worst of the road by building a flat boat to cross the river, which I intend to do next fall." (Reilly, 1999)

Hamblin did return the following year, but again used the upstream crossing at Ute Ford. He first attempted to cross in the fall of 1860 on a simple raft constructed at river's edge after a boat brought from Santa Clara, Utah was abandoned due to rough terrain. The raft couldn't carry much weight, however, and the party again headed for Ute Ford.

The usual purpose for these initial crossings of the Colorado River was for Mormon missionaries to meet with local Indian tribes inhabiting the region. The Church of Jesus Christ of Latter Day Saints believes that the native Americans of North America are of the blood of Israel. Great importance was placed on missionary work in this region. Also, with local Indians coming into the fold, Mormon expansion into central and southern Arizona would be greatly simplified.

The second reason for heading into the lands to the south was less spiritual. The first successful "boat" crossing of the river took place March 20, 1864 in an attempt to pursue Navajo raiders that regularly headed into lower Utah to steal cattle and horses. Jacob Hamblin and Lysander Dayton built a driftwood raft on-site and ferried fifteen men, animals and equipment across the river. It took two days. The party was less successful hunting marauding Navajos and returned to cross again on April 4.

The *Canyon Maid*, the first true boat used at Lee's Ferry, was put into service in October, 1870. A crude affair approximately twelve feet long with a three foot beam, its first trip was to take Jacob Hamblin and explorer John Wesley Powell across the river. Powell is best remembered for his trips down the Colorado River in 1869 and 1871. Between August and November of 1870 Powell was also engaged in an overland reconnaissance of southern Utah and northern Arizona for his second expedition through the Grand Canyon. Brigham Young traveled with the party and Powell engaged Jacob Hamblin to assist as guide and interpreter. Also joining the party for a portion of the trip was John Doyle Lee. A devout and zealous member of the Church, Lee had been involved in the notorious Mountain Meadows Massacre thirteen years earlier. Like everyone else involved, Lee had disappeared into rural southern Utah to avoid arrest. He was excommunicated, yet remained a faithful and committed Saint. However, political pressure to close the Mountain Meadows incident had been heating up. Church authorities realized the importance of keeping participants, including Lee, out of sight for their protection and the protection of the Church. It was on this expedition that the first mention of Lee being sent to the Colorado was made. Camped at the mouth of the Paria, Lee's diary entry for September 7, 1870 states:

"The Prest. (President Young) was well suited with the location. Asked me what I saw in that place that was of much benefit to us. I replied that I would want no greater punishment than to be sent on a Mission to the Pahariere. I would turn out Indian (i.e., become an Indian) at once & take no woman to such a Place." (Cleland, Brooks, 1983).

In November, 1871, Lee was officially sent to the crossing at the mouth of the Paria after a conference of Church leaders in St. George, Utah (at which Lee's fate was undoubtedly discussed). Lee was invited by Jacob Hamblin to settle at "Lonely Dell" as his partner. (The name "Lonely Dell" is often attributed to Lee's wife, Emma. However, Lee uses the name in his diary entry of November 15, 1870 before Emma had ever visited the area. Hamblin had probably named the place.) On Christmas Day, 1871, Lee arrived at the site that would bear his name with a company of nineteen people including his wives Rachel and Emma and thirteen children.

Lee became a ferryman on January 29, 1872 when a group of fifteen Navajos hailed him from the south side of the river. The only vessel at hand was the old *Canyon Maid* that was badly in need of caulking. His sons declined to cross in the perilous craft, but wife Rachel volunteered to steer as Lee rowed. The Indians brought a variety of goods to trade and Lee accommodated them, thereby becoming the first Indian trader at Lee's Ferry.

As government harassment grew over such issues as polygamy, the Mountain Meadows Massacre, and Church influence in territorial politics, Church officials saw the importance of establishing a dependable ferry capable of handling larger wagon trains. A larger ferry would permit Mormon expansion into the best locations in Arizona and would help improve the route to the south should a large exodus into Arizona or even Mexico become necessary. To these ends, construction of a boat for Lee's Ferry began in January, 1873. The vessel was twenty-six feet in length, eight and a half feet in beam and could hold one wagon and team. Named the *Colerado,* it was a vast improvement over the tiny *Canyon Maid*. Next, an approach to the ferry site had to be decided upon and improved. There were two possibilities for negotiating the horrendous terrain on the south side of the river. Lee's choice was a road over the long sloping bench of Shinarump Conglomerate directly across the river from the present launch ramp. Jacob Hamblin proposed a site downstream of the rapid at the mouth of the Paria. To Hamblin's chagrin, the upper site was selected because it afforded a

greater margin of safety before a boat would be swept irretrievably into the canyons below. The site's downside undoubtedly cursed by every traveler who ever used it. The arduous 600 foot climb and descent over "Lee's Backbone" is considered by some historians to be the worst piece of terrain ever routinely crossed by wagons.

The Mountain Meadows Massacre

As mentioned, the ferry site's namesake, first operator, and the region's first Indian trader was sent to the Colorado for his part in the Mountain Meadows massacre. Lee's role and conviction for the massacre makes interesting reading and is important sub-text to the history and settling of Lee's Ferry. It culminated on the blustery spring morning of March 23, 1877 when Lee sat quietly on his coffin, his sons on horseback in the distance, awaiting his execution. John Doyle Lee had been brought back to Mountain Meadows to single-handedly pay the price for the murder of over 120 people. Lee raised his hands over his head to allow an unobstructed shot. As five shots rang out, so ended one of the most bizarre episodes in the history of the American West.

The massacre for which Lee paid the ultimate price occurred on or about September 11, 1857, but the situations and tensions leading up to it had been building for some time. Throughout 1847 and 1848, thousands of Mormons fled Missouri and Illinois to avoid the persecution and harassment they had endured for years. They settled in the Salt Lake valley. The discovery of gold in California put them squarely in the path of the empire building to the west. Emigrants poured into Utah looking for supplies and a resting place before attempting the inhospitable deserts. These fortune hunters were polar opposites of the Saints who sought nothing more than a quiet, isolated place to raise families, practice agriculture and pursue their religious beliefs. As emigrants passed through the Utah territory, they rekindled the mistrust and hatreds of the past. Additionally, the federal government had become increasingly concerned over the practice of polygamy as well as the rise of a theocratic state in the territory of Utah. Here the Mormon Church, not Washington, exerted complete political and social control.

In 1857, the federal government sent a military force of 2,500 men into the territory to reestablish federal authority. Church leader Brigham Young and other Church officials inflamed the population, inciting the faithful to prepare for all-out war with the United States. The situation became known as the Utah War and although no lives were lost through military confrontation, reverberations of the conflict were to have dire consequences for the Baker-Fancher wagon train.

The Baker-Fancher party, about 140 men, women and children, mostly from Arkansas, was heading for southern California. The party encountered difficulties after leaving Salt Lake City. Church leaders had ordered that no aid be given to any emigrants passing through Utah during this time of "war". Shop owners refused to sell supplies to the party. The emigrants, for their part, did not act particularly responsibly, dare say intelligently, while passing through Mormon country. Alexander Fancher, an outspoken member of the group, had named his oxen after prominent Mormons such as Brigham Young and Heber C. Kimball. Another member boasted that he had the pistol that killed Church founder Joseph Smith at Carthage, Illinois in 1844. They also allegedly trampled crops, destroyed fences and poisoned water holes and livestock. They headed south to Mountain Meadows, just north of St. George, Utah, to camp and rest before crossing into the tortuous Nevada desert. (Lee, 1877)

With war looming with the U.S., Mormons secured Indian tribes as allies should a conflict erupt. Church authorities in the Cedar City area decided the best way to deal with the wagon train was to incite local Paiutes against them. This wasn't difficult as the party, like previous wagon trains, had shot any Indian they had come across. In his Church calling of Stake President, Isaac Haight sent John D. Lee to orchestrate the rallying of the Paiutes.

According to Lee, who was at his home in Harmony, the first attack on the Fancher party was waged early on a Tuesday morning by the Paiutes who didn't wait (per original plans) for reinforcements. The surprise attack from the hills to the east killed seven and wounded sixteen emigrants. Unfortunately for both the Paiutes and Lee, the emigrants quickly rallied and succeeded in repelling the attack, inflicting casualties. Later that morning Lee was notified and hastened to Mountain Meadows.

Now Lee was really in a jam. The Indians had been led to believe they could attack the emigrants without risk, yet had suffered casualties. They insisted Lee lead them to victory and that if he didn't they would attack Mormon settlements. Astonishingly, faced with 300 extremely agitated Indians, he convinced them to allow him to leave in order to bring back reinforcements. On the trail, he ran into a fully armed contingent of men heading for Mountain Meadows. According to Lee, they already knew what had happened and were determined to "obey orders." By Thursday night about fifty white men and about 400 Indians had gathered. (Lee, 1877)

On Wednesday evening three riders left the emigrant wagon train headed for Cedar City. One rider, William Aiden, having had previous dealings with the Mormons, was sent to secure cooperation against the savages. Young Aiden was ambushed by a white man; shot and killed while on his horse. His companions were then tracked and killed by Indians. Now it was possible the emigrants would know their assailants were white men. Should they escape, there would be certain cause for the United States army to ride into the Utah Territory from California. (Brooks, 1962)

On Thursday night a council was held and the following morning, under a white flag, William Bateman and Lee entered the emigrant camp. They proposed that, in exchange for protection from the Paiutes, the party surrender their arms and be escorted back to Cedar City. Those accused of misdemeanor crimes would face trial. Reluctantly, the desperate emigrants accepted the proposal. Lee later stated:

"I do not think there were twenty loads left in their whole camp. If the emigrants had had a good supply of ammunition, they never would have surrendered, and I do not think we could have captured them without great loss, for they were brave men and very resolute and determined." (Lee, 1877)

The youngest children – about seventeen in number – were loaded into one wagon, the wounded men into another. These wagons left camp and were followed a short distance by the women and older children. After a quarter of a mile, the men followed in single file, each emigrant man with an armed Mormon beside him. Then the order of "Do your duty!" was given. Each armed man turned and shot the emigrant next to him. Upon hearing the shots, Paiutes rushed from the bushes and killed all the women and older children. Witnesses stated it was over in less than five minutes. Later, Lee stated he was charged with killing the wounded in the wagon, but that his gun fired prematurely, slightly wounding a fellow Mormon.

Afterward, the younger children were farmed out to various families, the property was confiscated and all involved took a blood oath to never speak of the incident to anyone. The participants disappeared into life in the southern Utah frontier to live with the horror of what happened that day.

The massacre and exactly who was involved and to what extent has never been fully understood, nor will it ever be. The accounts in the two trials, nineteen years after the incident, were inconsistent. In the first trial, no Mormon would testify. The jury was undecided, with eight Mormons and one gentile for acquittal and three gentiles voting for conviction. Things changed at the second trial when Brigham Young ordered Mormon witnesses to testify. (Brooks, 1962) Five of these were at Mountain Meadows and it is likely most were more interested in saving their own skins than assuring justice. Furthermore, by the time of the trial Lee had been excommunicated from the Church. This fact would have most certainly implied guilt to Church members providing testimony and serving on the jury. Testimony pointed to Lee as the individual in charge at the massacre although various witnesses also stated other whites were involved. Brigham Young, who many stated under oath was not at the massacre, provided some of the most damaging testimony based on conversations he claimed he had with Lee. For this to be true, Lee had broken the oath of silence taken with the others in the massacre. Lee never testified at his trial. To the end he never denied having been involved but consistently stated that he was only following orders. Reading the transcripts of the trial, one becomes aware of the confused, chaotic and farcical nature of the proceeding.

Lee was sentenced to die and chose death by firing squad. In *Confessions of John D. Lee,* published after his death, Lee maintained innocence.

"I have acted as I was commanded to do by my superiors, and if I have committed acts that justify my execution, I ask my readers to say what should be the fate of the leaders in the Church who taught me to believe I could not and would not commit sin while obeying orders of the priesthood? My sins, if any, are the result of doing what I was commanded to do by those who were my superiors in authority."
(Lee, 1877)

Lee's membership in the Church was reinstated in 1961. A special marker was placed on his grave stating, "Ye Shall Know the Truth and the Truth Shall Make You Free." John 8:32

A New Ferryman Arrives

After Lee's arrest, Church authorities began searching for an individual to assist Emma Lee during her husband's absence. This was not an easy task as the isolation, intense and constant physical labor and danger associated with the outpost were well known. Warren M. Johnson was sent to Lee's Ferry in March, 1875. Emma Lee retained ownership of the ferry until May of 1879 when the Church bought the ferry rights for $3,000 paid mostly in cattle.

The ferry's first accident occurred May 24, 1876 when the river was high with spring runoff. For nearly a month, Johnson used a skiff to ferry passengers as the heavy, cumbersome ferryboat was unsafe during high flows. Using the skiff meant wagons had to be taken apart, sent across and reassembled. A delegation of Church dignitaries, on their way to settlements on the Little Colorado River, now found themselves on the bank of the swollen river. Johnson explained the hazard of using the large boat and that he would not be responsible under these conditions, but the group insisted they must cross the river by nightfall. He agreed to cooperate if the group appointed a temporary captain, and Bishop Lorenzo Roundy was selected. (The party included Apostles Brigham Young Jr., Erastus Snow, a number of Bishops, Jacob Hamblin and others.) To avoid being washed into the rapids downstream,

Emma Batchelor Lee moved to Lee's Ferry with her husband in December 1871. Known for her physical and emotional strength, Emma operated the ferry during her husband's long absences. In November of 1873, without medical help and single-handedly, Emma gave birth to a daughter, Victoria. Arizona Historical Society photo.

the boat was towed upstream with horses, then rowed across. This arduous procedure was repeated for two round trips before disaster struck when the fully loaded boat was being towed up the right bank. It washed against a boulder, forcing the inshore gunwale into the air and the opposite gunwale into the river, making the vessel roll over. Wagons and eight men were thrown into the river and Roundy was drowned. (Reilly, 1999)

In December of 1880, the Denver & Rio Grande Railway undertook a project to build a railway from Ogden, Utah to Arizona. In August of 1881, survey crews arrived to determine the best place for a bridge over the Colorado. In the course of their work, the problems with the current ferry site and crossing Lee's Backbone were obvious to the engineers. They discussed establishing their own ferry and excavating a dugway up the cliff face downstream of the Paria riffle, the site

Jacob Hamblin had wanted. Inspired by the possibility of the Church losing control of the crossing, Johnson told the engineers another crossing was already planned and that a crew was on the way. By November, 1881, a dugway had indeed been blasted into the Kaibab Limestone and a lower ferry site established. Now travelers arriving during periods of low water could avoid the trek over Lee's Backbone. This was the preferred ferry site for the next fifteen years. A short distance above the mouth of the Paria River, a large block of Kaibab Limestone lies in the middle of the Colorado. This rock became known as the "Gage Rock". When water poured over it, at a flow of approximately 43,000 cfs, it was time to change to the upper crossing. (Reilly, 1999)

Warren Johnson's term at Lee's Ferry ended in December of 1895, when Church authorities determined his mission was completed. He had transformed the remote and desolate corner into an abundant farm and operated the Ferry safely for over twenty years. During his tenure, the lower ferry site was established and a road circumventing the worst part of Lee's Backbone was built. Johnson was certainly the most dedicated operator of the ferry. Permanently paralyzed from a wagon accident in December, 1895, he moved with his families to Byron, Wyoming where he died March 10, 1902.

James Emett and A New Ferry

The early ferry boats were flat-bottomed barges of various sizes that were rowed across the river with sweeps. Occasionally, the barge was abandoned altogether and a small skiff was used. This meant that stock had to be swum across the river and wagons had to be dismantled and carried over a piece at a time. It seems strange that the idea of a track cable was not conceived until Johnson's replacement, James Emett, approached the Church with these improvements in February of 1898. Emett also proposed construction of a road, originally conceived by Johnson, that would parallel the river and lead to the upper ferry site, by-passing "Lee's Backbone". The plan was approved and work on the road began on January 30, 1899. Only ten to twelve feet wide and clinging precariously to the soft Moenkopi Shale cliff face, the road was subject to frequent washouts and rock falls. Sharlott Hall wrote of the dugway in 1911.

"This is a wonderful bit of road building; the old Mormon road went lower down but the river washed it away and the new road is slashed and carved out along places where it would make an eagle dizzy to fly; yet the work has been done so well that at least one automobile has come in over these terrific grades." (Hall, 1975)

While workers carved out the dugway, others were busy stringing the track cable at a point about a half-mile above the present launch ramp. The cable was attached to a rock outcrop on the south side, run over a tower of cribbed logs, and attached to a "deadman" on the north side. The ferry was attached to the cable fore and aft. Angling the boat in the current with the aid of a block and tackle drove the ferry one direction or the other. The road and cable-driven boat were completed in March, 1899. Although out of service for over seventy years, you can see the remnants of the dugway from the north side of the river.

The Polygamists

On October 6, 1890, Church President Wilford Woodruff took a step no previous Mormon had been willing to take and denounced plural marriage. This rocked the Church to its core and was the first reversal *ever* in church policy. It was the result of intense political pressure and federal legislation including the Edmunds Act of 1882 and the Edmunds-Tucker Act of 1887. These prohibited polygamy and unlawful cohabitation, barred practitioners from public service and voting and included provisions that could effectively destroy the Church. By 1890, over 12,000 Utah Mormons lost the right to vote. (Bradley, 1993) As virtually the entire Mormon hierarchy practiced "the Principle" the situation threatened to paralyze Mormon society. (Arrington, Bitton, 1979) The confusion, division and upheaval created by the Woodruff Manifesto cannot be overemphasized.

The tenant of plural marriage was central to Mormon doctrine, identity and solidarity and had far-reaching spiritual implications. Polygamy was not wrong, it became politically incorrect. No commentary was offered by Church authorities concerning the status of existing plural marriages. This threw many families into cruel dilemmas. The end of fifty-six years of Church condoned civil disobedience also created a conflict for the faithful between the laws of man and the laws of God. This gave rise to a fundamentalist sub-movement, which Salt Lake generally ignored as long as it was not blatantly causing the Church embarrassment. From 1909 to 1934, Lee's Ferry was home to a number of such fundamentalist families.

In 1909, the Grand Canyon Cattle Company bought the ferry from the Mormon Church. The cowboys working for the ranch were unwilling and poor ferry operators, so Jeremiah Johnson, son of former ferryman Warren Johnson, was contacted. Johnson, along with brothers Frank, Elmer and Price and their families, jumped at the chance to get back to the old family homesite. Jeremiah, the oldest and patriarchal figure of the clan, had struggled with the conflict surrounding plural marriage. After reading and rereading Wilford Woodruff's manifest, praying and fasting, he finally decided what others had also decided, that the decree was not divinely inspired and as such had nothing whatsoever to do with him. He would practice the tenant of plural marriage and in 1907, in spite of bitter opposition from his wife Annie, decided to take another bride. It was only Annie's death that prevented Jerry from committing bigamy.

Life at Lee's Ferry after the return of the Johnsons was a throwback to the 1880's, but without the prosperity. They endured the hard life at this remote outpost in exchange for practicing their religion as they believed. By 1923, Jerry had developed a vision of a pre-manifesto society to be built at the Lee's Ferry ranch. He convinced the Church that he and his brothers should purchase the ranch and operate the ferry as their father had. It is a testimony to the exemplary life of Warren Johnson that Church authorities agreed to provide a down payment of $4,000 to the Grand Canyon Cattle Company and put the ranch in Jerry's name. Jerry was to make subsequent payments and repay the original investment.

Other nonconformists eventually found their way to Lee's Ferry. Isaac Carling Spencer, Jeremiah's brother-in-law, moved one of his families there and helped raise the population of school-aged children to the minimum required to establish a school district. By 1925, Price and Elmer had second wives and in January of 1926,

Jerry was named presiding elder of the Lee's Ferry Branch of the Fredonia Ward. Rumors of blatant polygamy at Lee's Ferry circulated and on July 25, 1926 Jerry and Pearly Johnson and Elmer Johnson and his wives Viola and Artemisia were excommunicated. The Church paid off the Grand Canyon Cattle Company, as Jerry had been unable to meet his obligation. The Church now found itself in the embarrassing position of holding title to land being used by known excommunicated polygamists.

For the next eight years the Johnsons, Spencers and Grover Cleveland LeBaron and family lived as squatters on Church land, while the entire enterprise spiraled downward. Homesteading attempts failed, a service station at present day Vermilion Cliffs failed (in 1933) and eventually most moved away. Jerry's vision of a pre-manifesto communal society probably failed because of his inadequacies as a leader rather than from lack of interest. A number of his brothers and sisters joined the successful polygamist community at Short Creek, known today as Colorado City.

Charles Spencer

One of the more curious enterprises at Lee's Ferry was that of an energetic young engineer and promoter, Charles H. Spencer, who settled at Lee's Ferry in May of 1910. Spencer had been involved with a placer min-

The Charles H. Spencer, docked at Lee's Ferry in 1912. From left to right, Captain Pete Hanna, unidentified man, "Rip Van Winkle" Schneider, "Smitty" Smith, Jerry Johnson, Bert Leach and Al Byers. Photo courtesy of Emery Kolb collection, Cline Library, Northern Arizona University.

The Charles H. Spencer was the largest steamboat to operate on the Colorado River above the Grand Canyon. Photo courtesy of U.S. Geological Survey.

ing operation on the San Juan River, some 125 miles upstream of Lee's Ferry. The operation attempted to extract gold from the Wingate sandstone and was abandoned when the gold content proved too low and difficult to extract. At about this time, some of the best exposures of the easy-to-mine Chinle shale, believed to contain even more gold, were discovered at Lee's Ferry.

Spencer's plan was to use high-pressure hoses to wash the easily eroded shale over an amalgamator. Spencer also attempted to extract gold from river sediment using a suction dredge. During his 1911 trip, river runner Emery Kolb described this operation.

> *"One feature about the dredge interested us greatly. This was a tube, or sucker, held suspended by a derrick above a float, and operated by compressed gas. This tube was dropped into the sand at the bottom of the river and would eat its way into it, bringing up rocks the size of one's fist, along with the gravel and sand. In a few hours a hole, ten or fifteen feet in depth and ten feet in diameter, would be excavated. The tube was then raised, the float was moved and the work started again. The coarse sand and gravel, carried by a stream of water, was returned to the river after passing over the riffles; the screeing which remained, passed over square metal plates – looking like sheets of tin – covered with quicksilver. These plates were cleaned with a rubber window cleaner, and the entire residue was saved in a heavy metal pot, ready for the chemist." (Kolb, 1914)*

In the summer and fall of 1910, Spencer's men improved an old Indian trail to the top of the cliff face, northeast of the present parking lot. Climbing 1,600 feet in about a mile, it had probably been in use by white men for forty years but was inadequate for hauling coal, used to heat the boilers, from Warm Creek.

Spencer later claimed that his white mule, Pete, laid out the trail. "I just told him what to do and he started up the cliff. I followed him, marking the trail." While admitting Pete was a superior mule, none of the workman could later recall him having anything to do with laying out the trail. (Rusho, Crampton, 1992)

At American Placer Company's headquarters in Chicago, more grandiose minds planned another method to deliver the coal from Warm Creek. Against mild objection from Spencer, the corporate officers order a stern-wheel steamboat, the *Charles H. Spencer*. At eighty-seven and a half feet long and twenty-five feet wide, it was the largest vessel to operate upstream of the Grand Canyon. (Reilly, 1999) The $30,000 boat was constructed in San Francisco, disassembled, put on railroad cars and hauled to the railhead in Marysvale, Utah. Here the boat was loaded on wagons to begin the 200 mile trip to the Colorado River. This became even longer when the wagon carrying the boiler slipped off the road, sending the boiler seventy-five feet down an embankment. The workers spent a month getting it back out of the ravine and onto the wagon. (Rusho, Crampton, 1992) The components were eventually delivered to Warm Creek and reassembled.

At one point, Spencer noted that the smokestack of the sternwheeler was too high to pass under the cable at Lee's Ferry. It seems nobody considered mooring the boat upstream, so workmen began raising the cable. Unfortunately, nobody realized the importance of keeping it ninety degrees to the current and the anchor location on the south side was inadvertently moved about fifty feet upstream. On a northbound trip the ferry worked great. When heading south, excessive manpower was required to pull against the current. (Reilly, 1999)

In the spring of 1912, the steamboat was reassembled and ready for the voyage to Lee's Ferry. Coal had been stockpiled and loaded on a barge to be towed to the ferry. But wait. Nobody knew how to operate a steamboat. One man, Pete Hanna, had some experience of this kind and was conscripted as captain, at least for a short distance. Although Hanna had some boating experience, he evidently had little experience reading moving water. The boat ran hard aground just 100 yards from the launch and the crew spent the rest of the day digging her out with shovels.

The following day they again departed downstream with The *Charles H. Spencer,* making Lee's Ferry in a little over six hours. Before heading downstream, however, Captain Hanna attempted a short upstream run above Warm Creek. Operating under full steam, the boat managed to travel only 100 yards. It was apparent to the crew that they would be far too under-powered to push the empty barge back upstream to Warm Creek. Nothing had changed when it came time to make the attempt, except spring runoff, which made the river even higher and more powerful. Heading upstream from Lee's Ferry, they struggled for two hours without rounding the bend one and a half miles upstream. Although there are conflicting accounts, it is unlikely the boat ever made more than six trips to Warm Creek and, quite possibly, it never made even one return trip. It was moored about a quarter mile above the present Lee's Ferry boat ramp where a flood in 1915 washed driftwood up under the keel. When the water receded, the boat heeled over to one side and sank. (Reilly, 1999)

The chemists also had struggles extracting the gold from the Chinle shale. Something in the shale repeatedly fouled the amalgamation and the gold simply washed on through with the tailings. Samples were sent to chemists, including the famous Madam Curie in Paris. (Rusho, Crampton, 1992) Nobody could figure out what component of the formation wreaked havoc with the amalgamation process. This obstacle finally pulled the curtain on Spencer's Lee's Ferry mining operation. By 1913, the operation was abandoned, leaving the Spencer trail and *Charles H. Spencer* as interesting reminders of the ill-conceived endeavor.

Despite all this, the enterprise was not a complete failure. Spencer acted as custodian of the ferry under the employment of Coconino County. In March of 1912, after the futility of the mining enterprise had become apparent and Spencer found himself in financial difficulties, the miner billed the county for raising the cable so that his steamboat could pass underneath. They paid Spencer $841 for the work!

Ironically, the material that ruined the amalgamation process turned out to be rhenium. Highly valued today as a superconductor, it was entirely unknown in 1912. At over ninety years of age, Spencer returned to the area in 1962 and 1963 hoping to mine rhenium at still valid claims he held near the ghost town of Pahreah. He and his daughter performed tests on the shale but the idea never went any further. Spencer claimed his success was being blocked by international mining cartels that didn't want his vast body of ore to be put on the market. (Rusho, Crampton, 1992)

The Ferry's Last Trip and the Navajo Bridge

Forty-six years after the Denver & Rio Grande Railway surveyed for a railroad bridge, work commenced on a highway bridge at the very site chosen by these engineers. The bridge cost about $341,000 and was completed in eighteen months with but one serious accident. On June 12, 1928 steelworker Lafe McDaniels missed his footing and fell about 470 feet into the river. Safety nets were not installed because falling hot rivets, used in construction, would catch them on fire.

The previous week had seen another tragedy at the ferry crossing. On June 7, the river was running high, at about 85,600 cubic feet per second. Royce Deans,

an Indian trader from Cedar Ridge, and his Navajo helper Lewis (Nez) Tsinnie arrived at about noon returning from Kanab, Utah. Adolpha Johnson, the grandson of Warren Johnson, was operating the ferry. The party made the crossing without incident. As the boat nosed into the left bank, young Johnson jumped off and attempted to tie the boat to a post. A strong eddy current caught the boat and began to move it upstream and away from shore. Unable to hold the boat, Johnson was pulled into the river and climbed back aboard. The boat drifted under its own cable to the top of the eddy where it was pushed towards the main current. As it headed downstream, Johnson was unable to adjust the cables to gain the proper angle and the boat reached the end of the slack with a violent jerk. Taking the full force of the current broadside, the cables parted and the vehicle and all three men were thrown into the river. Johnson's wife Marva and their son Milo watched in horror from the shore. They never saw Adolpha or Deans again. Tsinnie was spotted floating motionless downstream. (Reilly, 1999)

This was the worst accident at the ferry and the last ferry trip. Since the bridge was near completion, county officials declined to spend the money to reestablish the ferry. For fifty-five years, boats traveling across the river at Lee's Ferry provided a vital link for travelers. It would be no more and from June 7, 1928 to January, 1929, there was no crossing the Colorado between Moab, Utah and Needles, California. When the bridge contractor had to move equipment or supplies to the other side of the 800 foot chasm, the only route was an eight hundred mile trip through Needles, California.

The Navajo Bridge before completion in January, 1929. The preceeding June, the ferry capsized, leaving bridge construction crews without a way to get materials and equipment to the other side of the 800 foot-wide chasm. The only solution was an 800 mile trip through Needles, California. Photo courtesy of Marble Canyon Company.

The new Navajo Bridge placed next to the original in 1995. The 1929 bridge serves as a pedestrian bridge. Photo by Dave Foster.

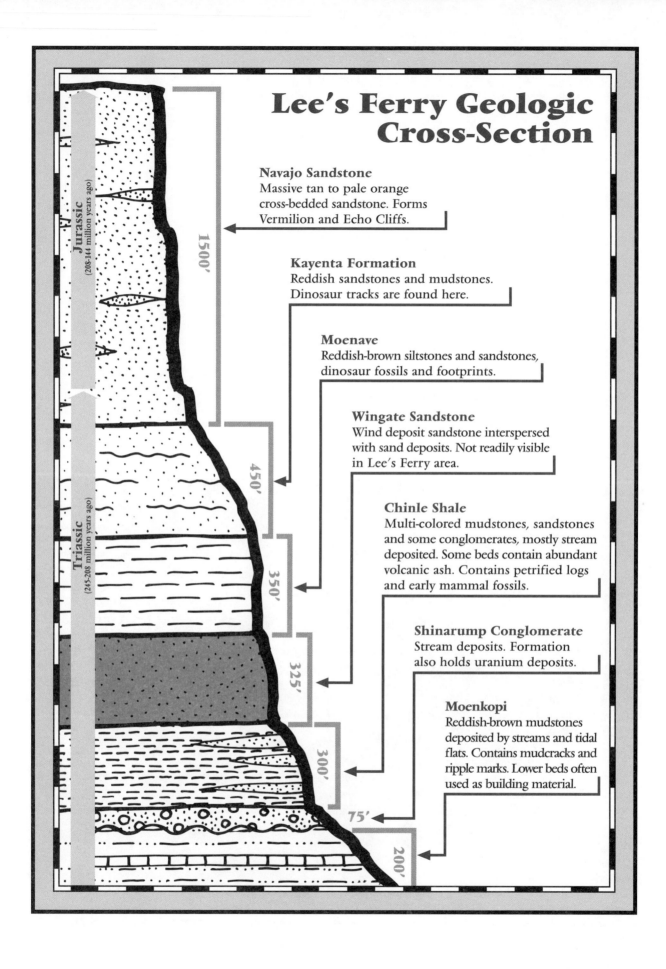

Lee's Ferry Geologic Cross-Section

Navajo Sandstone
Massive tan to pale orange cross-bedded sandstone. Forms Vermilion and Echo Cliffs.

Kayenta Formation
Reddish sandstones and mudstones. Dinosaur tracks are found here.

Moenave
Reddish-brown siltstones and sandstones, dinosaur fossils and footprints.

Wingate Sandstone
Wind deposit sandstone interspersed with sand deposits. Not readily visible in Lee's Ferry area.

Chinle Shale
Multi-colored mudstones, sandstones and some conglomerates, mostly stream deposited. Some beds contain abundant volcanic ash. Contains petrified logs and early mammal fossils.

Shinarump Conglomerate
Stream deposits. Formation also holds uranium deposits.

Moenkopi
Reddish-brown mudstones deposited by streams and tidal flats. Contains mudcracks and ripple marks. Lower beds often used as building material.

Jurassic (208-144 million years ago)

Triassic (245-208 million years ago)

1500'
450'
350'
325'
300'
75'
200'

Lee's Ferry Geology

Lee's Ferry is situated nearly in the center of one of the greatest geological showcases in the world, the Colorado Plateau geologic province. This area covers 130,000 square miles of the Four Corners Region and is characteristically high in elevation and composed of relatively flat lying sedimentary rocks. The Colorado Plateau has acted as a sort of geologic raft in a stormy sea. The region is surrounded by the geological chaos and deformation of the Rocky Mountains to the northeast and the Basin and Range geologic province to the west. Even though they have been uplifted as much as 10,000 feet, the rocks of the plateau have retained the horizontal position in which they were deposited. Each formation is representative of a chapter in the history of the earth. This wonderfully complete rock record has been exposed by erosion and reveals the events that formed the earth as we know it. From the 1.7 *billion* year old Vishnu Schist at the bottom of the Grand Canyon to the region's recent volcanic activity, the geology of the earth is here to be marveled at and unraveled.

To appreciate the geology of the Lee's Ferry area, it is helpful to understand some basic earth processes. For the most part, the rocks of the Colorado Plateau, including the Lee's Ferry area, are *sedimentary* rocks. Sedimentary rocks are secondary deposits, meaning the materials that form these rocks are the products of erosion. These materials were transported by water or wind and re-deposited to form the formations we see in the area today. This process of erosion and deposition is called the *rock cycle*.

The mechanics of the rock cycle work today as they have since the beginning of time. We can observe erosion and deposition today and use these observations to understand how rocks were deposited millions of years ago. This concept is called *uniformitarianism*. It holds that the present is the key to the past and that the laws of nature are invariable in their operation. A second important geologic principle is *superposition*. This holds that in any undeformed sedimentary sequence the oldest beds are on the bottom. The third basic geologic principle is *original horizontality*. This holds that sedimentary rocks are laid down flat or horizontally. If beds are upturned or tilted, they have been deformed after being deposited.

It should also be understood that different environments deposit different sedimentary rocks. Limestones, for instance, are often laid down in ocean basins far from where erosional debris from the continents enters the ocean via rivers. The material that will become shales is deposited closer to the continental source for these materials. Mudstones and siltstones may be deposited in tidal flats by low energy tidal currents. Along the coast, the coursest material is deposited in high energy beach environments as sandstones and conglomerates. This process by which material is separated by size is called *sorting*. Acknowledging the principle of uniformitarianism, we can observe beach and tidal environments today and understand the environments that deposited the rocks in the Lee's Ferry area millions of years ago. The material that makes up these rocks, as well as the cementing agents, determines how hard a formation is and how resistant it is to weathering. Hard rocks tend to erode to form vertical cliffs. Softer rocks erode to form gentle slopes. The principle that rocks erode at differing rates and form different features is called *differential erosion*. It is this principle that is responsible for much of the region's spectacular landscapes as well as the actual location of Lee's Ferry.

Geologically, Lee's Ferry is in a rather unique position along the Colorado River. For most of its journey across the Plateau, the Colorado has carved deep, inaccessible canyons through very hard, resistant formations. At Lee's Ferry the river encounters a flexure called the Echo Cliffs Monocline. This displacement has exposed a series of formations in rapid succession. Some of these formations are extremely soft and easily eroded. Where these rocks are at river level, such as at Lee's Ferry, no canyon is formed.

The rock formations exposed in the Lee's Ferry area had their genesis in the Triassic through the mid-Jurassic geologic periods, approximately 245-185 million years ago. This was the age of the dinosaurs when the seas retreated to the west and were replaced by lowlands and tidal flats. Some 4,000 to 8,000 feet of sediments were deposited in the region. As the sediments accumulated, the region subsided, resulting in little elevation gain relative to sea level. The oldest of these Triassic rocks is the *Moenkopi formation*, composed of muds and siltstones. This formation was deposited as tidal currents distributed stream sediments originating in highlands to the east. Exposures of Moenkopi closer to these source areas exhibit more stream or *fluvial* characteristics. In the area of Winslow, Arizona the Moenkopi is not well sorted and lacks the ripple marks and mudcracks associated with tidal flats. Northwest of Lee's Ferry, however, the formation becomes more well sorted and more marine in nature. Near Salt Lake City, these marine limestones thicken to 2,000 feet and dominate the foothills of the Wasatch range.

In the Lee's Ferry area, the Moenkopi forms the Chocolate Cliffs. These border Highway 89A from about fifty miles south of Lee's Ferry to the Kaibab Mountains twenty miles to the west. The lower beds of the Moenkopi, where it comes in contact with the marine Kaibab limestone, have supplied building material in the region for thousands of years, from early Anasazi pueblos to present day hotels. These transitional beds are high in calcium carbonate and are extremely hard. They are easily pried apart from intermittent shale and mudstone beds in beautiful, uniform slabs one to five inches thick.

The tidal environments ended when uplifting cut the region off from the seas to the west. Continental environments dominated the scene and a multitude of rivers flowed across the Colorado Plateau. These rivers deposited sand, silt and gravel that would become the *Chinle formation*, the lowest member of which is the *Shinarump Conglomerate*. Looking up at the Chocolate Cliffs, (see below) the Shinarump forms the vertical capstone at the top of the slope. The formation is a typical stream deposit consisting of unsorted material ranging in size from sand to cobbles. The Shinarump conglomerate was undoubtedly a source of chert that was fashioned into points and tools by ancient Indians inhabiting the area. The ancient streams also deposited large amounts of organic material in the form of logs,

sticks, twigs and leaves. This organic debris is an important component within the entire Chinle formation and is associated with the concentration and precipitation of uranium minerals. It is not wholly understood what mechanisms brought uranium rich fluids to the region, but uranium deposits are dated approximately 150 million years younger than the rocks in which they are found. It has been speculated that uranium rich fluids migrated through the Chinle until coming in contact with organic material which acted to localize uranium minerals. It was the Shinarump that brought uranium prospectors to the area in the 1940's.

The main body of the Chinle is made up of multicolored shales with a few thin beds of fluvial sandstones and limestones probably deposited in lakes. The region must have been a nearly flat plane for such extensive river and lake deposits to accumulate. Chinle shale forms the Painted Desert and the badlands country of the Cameron-Winslow-Holbrook-Sanders region in Arizona. There are also petrified logs in the Chinle, with the greatest concentrations being near Holbrook, Arizona at Petrified Forest National Park.

Petrification of logs occurs when silica rich waters permeate the pores in woody tissue. Organic material is completely infilled and encased in silica, not replaced or changed to rock. The structure of the original material is perfectly preserved. The bright colors are caused by iron impurities within the silica. There is a fifty foot

View of Lee's Ferry boat ramp and parking. Across the river is Lee's Backbone, the large bench rising left to right. Photo by Dave Foster.

Diagonal patterns in Navajo sandstone formed by windblown sand deposits. Photo by Dave Foster.

primarily of fluvial sandstones and mudstones. The alteration of these units produces a series of ledges and forms a blocky, horizontally bedded, reddish brown cliff between the Moenave and Navajo sandstone. Dinosaur tracks are sometimes found in the Kayenta.

The towering cliffs of Glen Canyon between Lee's Ferry and the dam are composed of *Navajo Sandstone*. In the Lee's Ferry area the Navajo Sandstone is 1,400-1,700 feet thick and exhibits classic examples of high angle, large scale crossbeds in conspicuous, wedge-shaped sets. The Navajo sandstone is mostly fine, uniform grains of pure quartz sand and also contains thin beds of fresh water limestones indicating the presence of seasonal lakes or *playas*. Thin limestone beds can be seen in Glen Canyon at Six Mile Bar and Duck Island. In Glen Canyon the walls are also decorated with *desert varnish*. Heading upstream, look for the distinctive, shiny, gunmetal blue-black patches on the canyon walls. This veneer is primarily iron and manganese oxide. Desert varnish develops slowly, over many centuries. Although not fully understood, it is likely formed by minerals gradually leached from the rock or from soluble material carried in dust and spread thinly and repeatedly by occasional rainwater.

petrified log on the sloping surface of the Shinarump Conglomerate (Lee's Backbone) directly across from the Lee's Ferry boat ramp.

Towards the end of the Triassic period, the environment of the Colorado Plateau region began to change again. A great Sahara-type desert began to form and eventually covered at least two thirds of the region. The rocks of the *Glen Canyon Group* preserve this transition. *Wingate Sandstone* is the lowest member of the Glen Canyon Group and is composed mostly of sandstones exhibiting the high angle crossbeds characteristic of wind or *aolian* deposits. These beds are occasionally interspersed with the low angle crossbedded deposits characteristic of streams. This indicates the environment at the time varied at least seasonally. The Wingate Sandstone is not readily visible in the Lee's Ferry area. Above the Wingate is the *Moenave formation* composed primarily of siltstones and sandstones and is representative of sediments deposited by stream systems over low lying land. It is approximately 350 feet thick in the Lee's Ferry area and is various shades of red, orange and reddish brown.

In the area of Tuba City, Arizona, the Moenave formation has yielded the bones of dinosaurs and of tritylodon, one of the earliest mammal-like creatures. Above the Moenave is the *Kayenta formation* composed

Wind and water eroded Navajo sandstone at Nine Mile campground. Photo by Dave Foster.

High scalers at work at Glen Canyon Dam site. Photo courtesy of US Department of the Interior, Bureau of Reclamation.

Glen Canyon Dam

Glen Canyon Dam rises from the emerald green waters of the Colorado River 15.5 miles upstream from Lee's Ferry. Finished in 1963 after seven years of construction, the dam stands 600 feet above the riverbed and consists of ten million tons of concrete aggregate. Behind it stretches 186 miles of Lake Powell that contains twenty-seven million acre feet (maf) or nine trillion gallons of water. In front of it lies one of the most controversial rivers of the west.

Today's operation of Glen Canyon Dam is the result of a snarled array of legal, political, economic, environmental and climactic constraints and influences that are outside the scope of this book. Understanding the rudiments of some of these relationships, however, will help anglers understand the daily and seasonal river fluctuations and their effects on the Lee's Ferry fishery. This begins with the Colorado River Compact of 1922.

This plan established the Compact Point one mile below the mouth of the Paria River and allocated water to states above and below the point. River water goes to the upper basin of Colorado, Wyoming, Utah and New Mexico and the lower basin of Arizona, Nevada and California. Using the average runoff from 1906-1922 of fifteen maf a year, the plan directed the upper basin provide 7.5 maf to lower basin states. Water wasn't directed to Mexico, however, creating tension that resulted in the Mexican Water Treaty of 1944 and an allotment of 1.5 maf. This was to be split by the upper and lower basin states. The upper basin deducts the contribution of the Paria River (entering just below Lee's Ferry and contributing roughly 0.75 maf a year), thus downstream commitments require a minimum of 8.2 maf go past Lee's Ferry each year.

To regulate lower basin water delivery, Glen Canyon Dam was authorized by the Colorado River Storage Plan in 1956. The Colorado River Basin Act of 1968 reaffirmed the dam's purposes and includes this passage.

"This program is declared to be for the purposes, among others, of regulating the flow of the Colorado River; controlling floods; improving navigation; providing for the storage and delivery of waters of the Colorado River for reclamation of lands including supplemental water supplies, and for municipal, industrial, and other beneficial purposes; improving water quality; providing for basic public outdoor recreation facilities; improving conditions for fish and wildlife, and the generation and sale of electrical power as an incident of the foregoing purposes."

Glen Canyon Dam foundation preparation with dam bridge in place. Bureau of Reclamation photo.

In 1977, the Western Area Power Administration (WAPA) assumed responsibility for brokering and distributing Glen Canyon Dam power. In spite of the provisions of the Colorado River Basin Act, power generation became the dominant factor influencing releases from the dam. Glen Canyon Dam operates as a peaking power or load following facility, as opposed to a base load facility. Base load facilities, such as coal fired power plants, take twenty-four hours to reach full gen-

Glen Canyon Dam today. Photo by Dave Foster.

Early dam construction, late 1950's. Bureau of Reclamation photo.

erating capacity. Hydro-facilities by contrast, can reach full capacity in minutes, allowing additional generation at peak demand times when prices are highest. WAPA's dedication to marketing peak demand hydropower resulted in radical flow regimes and significant negative impacts on downstream environments. In 1983, the Bureau of Reclamation began the most ambitious ecological research project ever attempted by the United States government downstream of the dam.

The Glen Canyon Environmental Study (GCES) was a cooperative research venture including the National Park Service, Bureau of Reclamation, U.S. Fish and Wildlife Service, U.S. Geological Survey and the Arizona Department of Game and Fish. The project was a monumental undertaking investigating the impact of dam operations on existing environmental and recreational resources in Glen and Grand Canyons. The project was also to determine if modifications to dam operations could reduce such impacts. The project was made more difficult because pre-dam baseline data was almost nonexistent. At times the studies themselves were responsible for significant impacts. Extremely low flows permitted aerial photography and other projects June 1990 - July 1991. This destroyed much of the forage base in the Lee's Ferry reach, making the trout population crash and leaving the surviving fish in poor shape. For a time, the fishery was reduced to a mere glimmer of its former self.

This project did bring to light the concept that the dam might operate for something other than electric power, and confirmed what many suspected: fluctuating load-following flows implemented by WAPA had significant impacts on many of the downstream resources. In 1989, the Secretary of the Interior deemed an Environmental Impact Statement on dam operation necessary. As part of this process, data from the GCES was used to formulate interim flows designed to protect natural resources in Glen and Grand Canyons. These flows were implemented in August of 1991 and,

as far as the trout fishery was concerned, began the process of recovery after years of destructive peaking power and test flows.

The Grand Canyon Protection Act of 1992 directs that Glen Canyon Dam operate to protect and lessen adverse impacts and to improve the values for which Grand Canyon National Park and Glen Canyon National Recreation Area were established. This includes, but is not limited to, natural and cultural resources and visitor use. While still operated as a load-following facility, flow regimes must fall within strict parameters.

The Impressive Dam

Seeing Glen Canyon Dam from downstream for the first time inspires awe and a touch of apprehension at the magnitude and incongruity of the structure. This manmade feature rivals the region's natural wonders for visual impact. The hum of the generators, as falling water is turned into electricity, is heard a half-mile away and the river bubbles lazily, cold and green, from beneath the monolith. The dam produces four billion kilowatt hours of electricity per year, serving the needs of two million people. And yes, the dam leaks. Water streams down the canyon walls below it, watering fern gardens hanging high above the river. Closer to the dam you will see hundreds of stabilizing rods driven into the peeling sandstone to hold it in place. For all the size, strength and generating capacity of this manmade marvel, the relentless forces of nature will eventually

Pouring concrete into forms, showing penstocks in place. Bureau of Reclamation photo.

84

remove it. In the meantime, the dam continues to have a significant impact on the Colorado River below.

Flow Volume Changes

Before the dam, river flows varied seasonally with high flows in late spring and summer followed by low flows in the late summer, fall and winter. Peak flows usually occurred in June and ranged from 30,000 cubic feet per second (cfs) during low run-off years to well over 100,000 cfs during peak years. Annual low flows generally ranged from 3,000 cfs to 8,000 cfs. Every ten years or so, a flood of at least 120,000 cfs ripped through the canyons. The highest recorded flow was 200,000 cfs measured in 1921. In the spring of 1884, following the extremely severe winter of 1883-1884, the river rose to levels not seen before or since. Some speculate that the huge amounts of volcanic ash sent into the atmosphere by the eruption of the Krakatoa volcano may have produced a short-lived global cooling. Ferryman Warren Johnson noted river water almost reached his house, about a mile up the Paria Canyon from the main river. The river peaked at an estimated 300,000 cfs!

Temperature Changes

Not only were pre-dam flows highly variable, so were the water temperatures. The midwinter pre-dam Colorado ranged from just above freezing to about 40 degrees. At least five times, in 1866, 1878, 1879, 1912 and 1925, the river was frozen bank to bank to a thickness that allowed men and animals to cross. During spring runoff, water temperatures warmed to 60-70 degrees and peaked at 75-85 degrees by the end of August.

Now, water that leaves Glen Canyon Dam comes from 200 feet below the surface of the lake and is well within the hypolimnion (water that is below the layer warmed by sunlight). River water temperatures stay around 48 degrees year-round. Slight variations occur when the lake turns over, usually in December. This event may increase water temperatures below the dam a degree or two. As it travels downstream, the river warms an average of one degree every twenty miles traveled. High flows tend to warm less because water moves through the system quickly, while low flows tend to warm more. During most of the summer of 2000 a constant flow of 8,000 cfs was maintained and in the uncirculated backwaters and eddies in Glen Canyon, temperatures warmed into the 70's. The flowing water of the main current remained cold.

Changes in the Sediment Load

Perhaps the most significant change the dam created, from a biological standpoint, has been the reduction of sediment load. Between 1926 and 1950 the Colorado transported an average of 168 million *tons* of sediment past Phantom Ranch each year. (Thomas, Gould, Langbein, 1960) This was highly variable. On one record-breaking day during the great flood of 1927, an estimated 27 million tons of sediment was carried past Phantom Ranch. Today's reduced sediment load is about 14 million tons a year, and comes mostly from the Paria and Little Colorado rivers. The stretch between Lee's Ferry and the dam has no year-round tributaries and is essentially clear of suspended material.

This reduction of sediment load has also affected the river bottom (or substrate). Pre-dam floods carried unbelievable amounts of sediment that were deposited when the floods subsided. This created a constantly shifting sand and silt bottom, like the shifting dune sands of a Sahara-type desert and with about the same amount of biological activity. By contrast, the most productive river bottoms are composed of cobbles and gravel. With reduced silt, the river removed the finer sediments, leaving the cobble/gravel substrate that exists in the Lee's Ferry stretch today.

Construction of the east spillway, Glen Canyon Dam. Bureau of Reclamation photo.

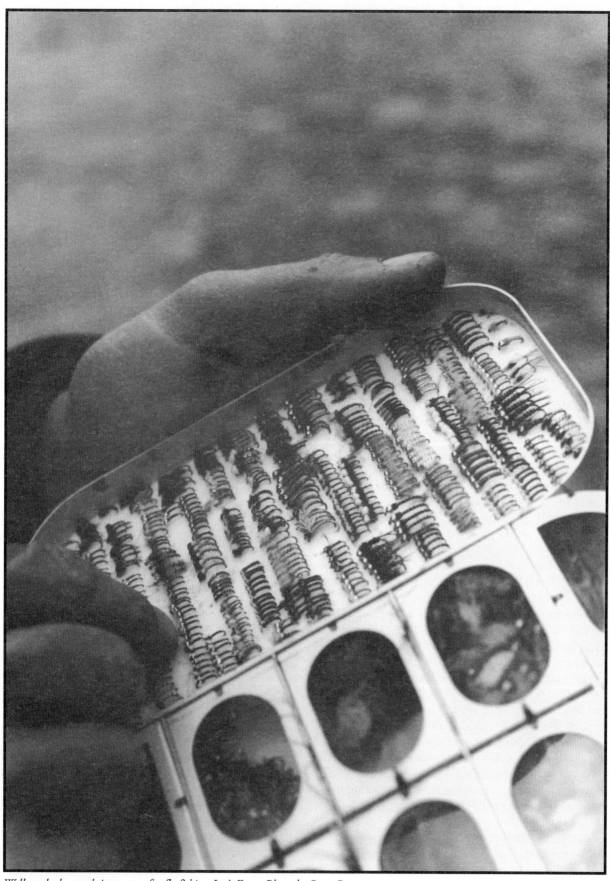

Well stocked nymph inventory for fly fishing Lee's Ferry. Photo by Scott Baxter.

Appendix

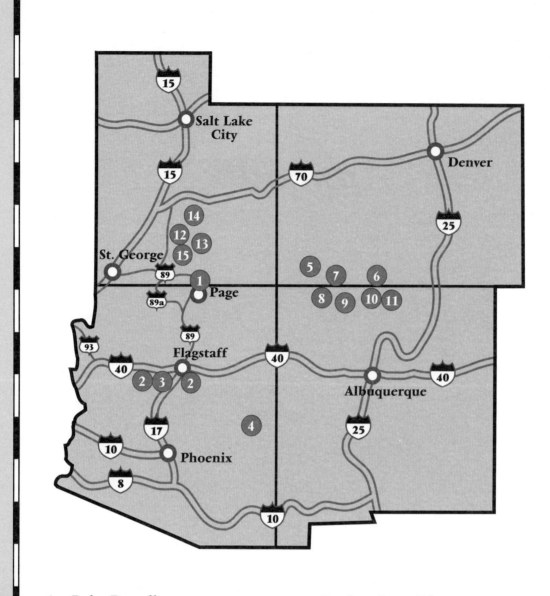

1. Lake Powell
2. Upper & Lower Lake Mary
   JD Dam Lake
3. Oak Creek
4. White Mountain Area
5. Animas River
6. Conejos River
7. Piedra River
8. San Juan River
9. Upper Chama
10. Los Pinos/Cruces Basin
11. Rio Costilla
12. Antimony Creek
13. Boulder Mountain, East
14. Fremont River
15. Pine Lake

Nearby Fly Fishing

Many anglers, traveling by car, break up their trip and get in a little fly fishing en route to Lee's Ferry. In some cases there is not much fishable water to work with (for example, the trip from Las Vegas to Lee's Ferry). In fact, in some stretches there is not much water, period. Thankfully, one can find fly water in most of the "Four Corner" states.

For the waters listed here, you can get by with the same gear you packed for Lee's Ferry. In all fairness, however, and to be precise, for trout angling these waters you should have a three to six weight rod, 7' to 9'. A palm drag or click reel is fine, as is floating line. Bring 4x - 5x, 71/2' to 9' leaders. For wading, chest-high neoprene or micro-fiber waders and boots will work for most all waters. You can use hip boots or wet-wade many waters in the heat of summer. For bass and big fish on Lake Powell up-size your rod and leaders or use what you packed for Lee's Ferry.

The best way to select flies for this region is to ask a local fly shop (listed after each water). Bring these basics and you will be ready for most of these waters.

Dries: Elk Hair Caddis, Blue Winged Olive #14-18, Parachute Adams, Hoppers #12-20.
Nymphs & Streamers: Black Woolly Bugger, Olive Crystal Bugger, Muddler Minnow #4-10, Peacock #8-14, Beadhead Hare's Ear #12-18, Poundmeister #8-10, Olive, Brown Damselfly.
Bass & Stripers: Poppers, Clouser Minnows, Deceivers.

Arizona

1. Lake Powell

Powell is 160,000 acres huge and best covered with a bass boat. Find fishy cover in coves and drop-offs. Look for striped bass chasing shad. You can also fish for largemouth and smallmouth bass, crappie, carp, walleye, pike and sunfish. Access Lake Powell from the town of Page, AZ. Marble Canyon Outfitters (800) 533-7339, Mike Ritz (928) 645-2287, Stix Bait & Tackle (928) 645-2891.

2. Upper & Lower Lake Mary and JD Dam

Not scenic places to fish but trout and pike are available if you are in the area at the right time of day. Fish the weed beds and underwater structure from a kick boat. Floating lines work well during hatches. Try grasshopper patterns too. Babbits, Flagstaff (520) 779-3235, Lynx Creek Unlimited, Prescott (520) 776-7088, Lake Mary Boat Rentals, Flagstaff (520) 774-1742.

3. Oak Creek

Traveling Highway 89? Just north of the town of Sedona there is access to several miles of fishable water with good trout in the upper canyon section. Fish a large attractor dry fly or hopper on top. Tie a Hare's Ear or Pheasant Tail nymph about 20" below. Most use Beadheads. Use a #20 Adams Parachute for the afternoon baetis hatch. Use Woolly Buggers in deep pools and under banks for large browns. Babbits, Flagstaff (520) 779-3253, Lynx Creek Unlimited, Prescott (520) 776-7088.

4. White Mountain Area

Fish for Apache, rainbow and brown trout and try the Black River, Crescent Lake, Earl Park Lake, the Little Colorado River, the many White Mountain Lakes and the White River. Mountain Outfitters, Pinetop (502) 367-6200, Skier's Edge, Pinetop (520)367-6200.

Colorado

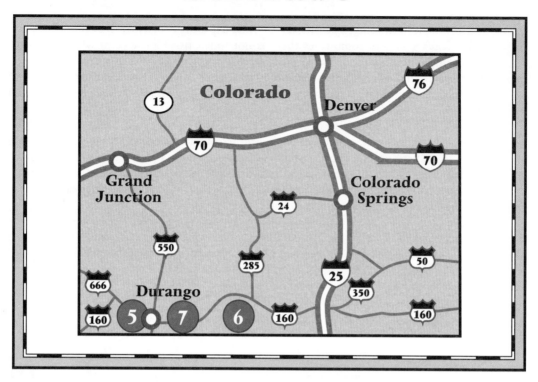

Colorado

5. Animas River

The upper river is in a scenic canyon and has fast riffles and pools. Through and below Durango there are eight miles of the best water including a gold medal stretch between Lightner Creek and the "Purple Cliffs". Browns and rainbows 18" - 20" are available. Best times to fish are February – April and July – November. Duranglers, Durango (970) 385-4081, Durango Fly Goods (970) 259-0999, Gardenschwartz Sporting Goods (970) 247-2660, Animas Valley Anglers (970) 749-3474.

6. Conejos River

In a lovely pine and canyon setting, fish over sixty miles of water for wild trout and even some northern pike. River access is easy and one can wade most all sections of the fifty foot wide river. Dan's Fly Shop, Lake City (970) 944-2281, Durango Fly Goods, Durango (970) 259-0999, Duranglers (970) 385-4081.

7. Piedra River

East of Durango on Highway 160 there is a section of public access, or head to Sheep Springs off the country road running next to the river. Either place offers great wild trout with lots of pools, riffles, and slow dry-fly sections. The Sportsman, Lake City (970) 944-2526, Dan's Fly Shop, Lake City (970) 944-2281, Durango Fly Goods, Durango (970) 259-0999, Duranglers (970) 385-4081.

Information and help comes from the No Nonsense Fly Fishing Guidebooks series (www.nononsenseguides.com). Thanks to contributing authors, Jackson Streit (CO), Taylor Streit (NM), Steve Schmidt (UT) Glenn Tinnin (AZ) and editor & publisher David Banks. Maps by Pete Chadwell.

New Mexico

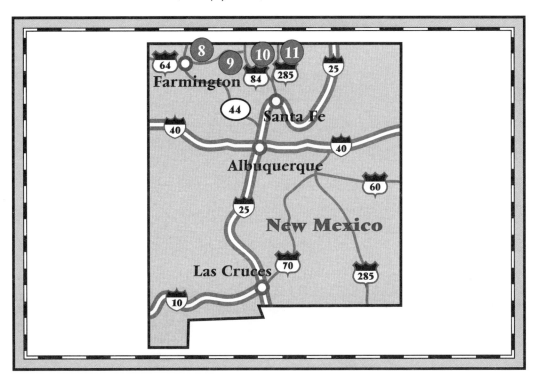

New Mexico

8. San Juan River

New Mexico's premiere fly fishing destination for tiny flies, light tippets and big fish. Most drift nymphs along the bottom, though there is excellent sight fishing using dry flies. Bring waders and warm clothes, as the water is rather cold. Lots of access. Fox Creek Store, Antonito, CO (719) 376-5881, Abe's Motel & Fly Shop, Navajo Dam, NM (505) 632-2194, New Sportsman Inn, Navajo Dam (505) 632-3271, Rizuto's Fly Shop, Navajo Dam (505) 632-3893.

9. Upper Chama

Usually best July 1 to early October. Go to Wolf Creek just above the town of Chama for a rugged walk in and fish from the west side of the river. Excellent for big fish. For easier dry fly fishing, go just below Chama for parking and river access. Los Rios Anglers, Taos, NM (505) 758-2798, Starr Angler, Red River, NM (505) 754-2320, Williams Trading Post, Red River (505) 754-2217.

10. Los Pinos / Cruces Basin

A long drive from anywhere, but the angling is worth it. This gem of a stream is seldom over waist deep and has perfect dry fly water. A scenic railroad parallels the water by Osier station into New Mexico. The Cruces Basin Wilderness Area features a long, dusty ride, brook trout, three creeks, waterfalls, beaver ponds and solitude. This is time-consuming country to fly fish, but worth it. Los Rios Anglers, Taos, NM (505) 758-2798, Starr Angler, Red River, NM (505) 754-2320, Williams Trading Post, Red River (505) 754-2217.

11. Rio Costilla

Another long drive from anywhere, but uncrowded. Go four miles past Latir Creek for the best water. Farther upstream in the meadows of the Valle Vidal unit is the most popular section. Fish for cutthroat with a big dry fly and a small beadhead nymph tied 18" below. Friday - Sunday the water is low and best for fly fishing. Other times, flows are high for irrigation so stick to edges and slower pools. Try nearby Little Camanche creek for dry fly action. Cottonwood Meadows, Antonito, CO (719) 376-5660, Hi Country Flies, Trinidad, CO (719) 846-6900, Los Rios Anglers, Taos, NM (505) 758-2798.

Utah

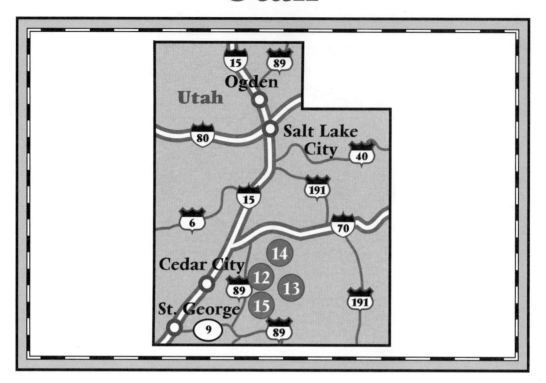

Utah

12. Antimony Creek

A beautiful little freestone stream with cool riffles and deep, clear pools. There is great dry fly fishing using size #16-18 patterns and small rods for wild, 10" - 16" trout. An OK dirt road leads to Antimony but fish the stream after the confluence with Poison Creek and the Sevier River, just after it exits the USFS boundary line. Take the trail up a narrow sandstone canyon, a very pleasant hike. Red Rocks Fly Shop, St. George, UT (435) 656-4665, Boulder Mt. Fly Fishing, Boulder, UT (435) 335-7306.

13. Boulder Mountain, East Side

Use scenic Highway 12 to get to Long Lake and Oak Creek Reservoir as well as trailhead access for hikes to several other lakes. Four-wheel drive is recommended on Road 179 to Green Lake or the trailhead to Blind Lake where six pound splake have been caught. Several other lakes are within thirty to ninety minute hikes. Off Road 521, (also 4WD) find access to Coleman and Round lakes and trailheads to several other waters. Boulder Mt. Fly Fishing, Boulder, UT (435) 335-7306, Red Rocks Fly Shop, St. George, UT (435) 656-4665.

13. Fremont River

The upper Fremont, below Fish Lake and Johnson Reservoir, offers nine miles of fishing along scenic Highway 25. Curves, deep holes and undercuts hold naturally reproducing brown trout. Easy access can mean many anglers. For the best dry fly fishing, head south of the town of Bicknell, just east of the Egan Fish Hatchery. Here, open and slow moving, very clear water requires a stealthy approach. Western Rivers Flyfishers, Salt Lake City, UT (800) 545-4312, Red Rocks Fly Shop, St. George, UT (435) 656-4665, Boulder Mt. Fly fishing, Boulder, UT (435) 335-7306.

14. Pine Lake

Take Highway 12 near Bryce Canyon National Park to Highway 63 and head north on Jones Valley Road. The pavement ends and you reach FR 132 where you will take a right. Use a float tube, canoe, or small boat, especially mid-day. Fish dropoffs, ledges, and floating weed beds. Match Damselflies, dragonflies, callibaetis, midges, water boatmen, leeches, and scuds. Boulder Mt. Fly Fishing, Boulder, UT (435) 335-7306, Western Rivers Flyfishers, Salt Lake City, UT (800) 545-4312, Red Rocks Fly Shop, St. George, UT (435) 656-4665.

References

Gosse, JC, *Preliminary Investigation of Microhabitats for Plants Macroinvertebrates and Fish in the Colorado River Below Glen Canyon Dam, with regard to peaking,* Report to U.S. Fish and Wildlife Service, Phoenix, AZ (1981)

Maddux, HR, et.al., *Effects of varied flow regimes on aquatic resources of Glen and Grand Canyons,* Final report to U.S. Department of the Interior (1987)

McKinney, T and Persons, WR, *Rainbow Trout and Lower Trophic Levels in the Lee's Ferry Tailwater Below Glen Canyon Dam* (AZ, March, 1999) p. 14

Reger, S, Benedict, C, Niccum, J, Magnuson, Y, Ayers, A, and Persons, WR, *Colorado River Lee's Ferry Fish Management Report, 1994-1997.* (In house report AZ Game and Fish Department, 1997)

James, George Wharton, *In and Around the Grand Canyon. The Grand Canyon of the Colorado River in Arizona* (Boston, Little, Brown and Company, 1942) p. 352

Reilly, PT, *Lee's Ferry, from Mormon Crossing to National Park* (Logan, Utah State University Press, 1999) p. 4

Cleland, R and Brooks, J, ed. *A Mormon Chronicle: The Diaries of John D. Lee 1848-1876* (Salt Lake City, University of Utah Press, 1983) p.138

Lee, JD, *Mormonism Unveiled or the Life and Confessions of the Late Mormon Bishop John D. Lee* (St. Louis, Bryan, Brand & Company, 1877) pp. 280-281

Lee, JD, *ibid*, p. 220

Brooks, J, *The Mountain Meadows Massacre* (Norman, University of Oklahoma Press, 1962) pp. 70, 72

Lee, JD, *ibid*, p. 240

Brooks, J, *ibid*, p.197

Lee, JD, *ibid*, p. 36

Reilly, PT, *ibid*, pp. 65-67

Reilly, PT, *ibid*, p. 98

Bradley, Martha S, *Kidnapped from That Land* (Salt Lake City, University of Utah Press, 1993.) pp. 10-11

Arrington, LJ, and Bitton, D, *The Mormon Experience: A History of the Latter-day Saints* (New York, Alfred A. Knopf, 1979) p. 204

Kolb, EL, *Through the Grand Canyon from Wyoming to Mexico* (New York, The Mcmillan Company, 1914) p. 173

Rusho and Crampton, *Lee's Ferry, Desert River Crossing* (Salt Lake City, Cricket Productions, 1992) p. 70

Reilly, PT, *ibid*, p. 448. (In some accounts, the boat was erroneously reported as 92 feet long.)

Rusho and Crampton, *ibid*, p. 72

Reilly, PT, *ibid*. p. 252

Rusho and Crampton, *ibid*. p. 69

Rusho and Crampton, *ibid*. p. 79

Reilly, PT, *ibid*, p. 216

Hall, S, edited by Gregory Crampton, *Sharlot Hall on the Arizona Strip* (Northland Press, 1975) p. 52

Reilly, PT, *ibid*. p. 329

Thomas, HE, Gould, HR and Langbein, WB, *Life of a Reservoir, in W.O. Smith et al. Comprehensive Survey of Sedimentation in Lake Mead, 1948-49.* U.S. Geol. Survey Prof. Paper 295-T (U.S. Gov't. Printing Office, Washington, 1960) pp. 231-248

Resources

Arizona Fly Shops

Alta Vista Anglers
4730 N. 7th Ave.
Phoenix, AZ 85013
(602) 277-3111

Arizona Fly Fishing
31 W. Baseline Rd.
Tempe, AZ 85283
(480) 730-6808
www.azflyfishing.com

Babbits
15 East Aspen Ave.
Flagstaff, AZ 86001
(520) 779-3253

Don's Sport Shop
7803 E. McDowell Rd.
Scottsdale, AZ 85257
(800) 637-7411
www.donsportshop.com

Dry Creek Outfitters
5420 E. Broadway Ste 254
Tuscon, AZ 85711
(520) 32-ORVIS
www.orvistuscon.com

Lee's Ferry Anglers
Milepost 547 N. Hwy 89A
HC-67 Box 30
Marble Canyon, AZ 86036
(800) 962-9755
www.leesferry.com

Lynx Creek Unlimited
130 W. Gurly Street, Ste. 307
Prescott, AZ 86301
(520) 776-7088

Marble Canyon Outfitters
PO Box 6032
Marble Canyon, AZ 86036
(800) 533-7339
www.leesferryflyfishing.com

Mountain Outfitters
560 W. White Mountain Blvd.
Pinetop, AZ 85935
(520) 367-6200

On The Creek, Sedona Outfitters
274 Apple Ave. Suite C
Sedona, AZ 86336
(928) 203-9973

Scottsdale Fly Fishing
10050 N. Scottsdale Rd. Ste. 101
Scottsdale, AZ 85253
(602) 368-9280
www.worldflyfish.com

The Speckled Trout
224 E. Main St.
Springerville, AZ 85938
(928) 333-0852
www.cybertrails.com/~cltrout

Tight Lines
4444 E. Grant Rd., Ste.113
Tucson, AZ 85712
(520) 322-9444

Wager's Fly Shop
1 South Main
Cottonwood, AZ 86326
(520) 639-2022

California Fly Shops

Bob Marriott's Fly Fishing Store
2700 W. Orangethorpe
Fullerton, CA 92833
(714) 578-1747
www.bobmarriotts.com

Colorado Fly Shops

Duranglers
923 Main Street
Durango, CO 81301
(888) 347-4346
www.duranglers.com

Mountain Angler
311 South Main
Breckenridge, CO 80424
800-453-4669
www.mountainangler.com

Nevada Fly Shops

Clear Water Fly Fishing
3031 E. Charleston Road #D
Las Vegas, NV 89104
(702) 388-1022

Las Vegas Fly Shop
7520 Washington Ave. #140
Las Vegas, NV 89128
(702) 838-6669
www.lasvegasflyshop.com

New Mexico Fly Shops

Los Pinos Fly Shop
2820 Richmond Drive NE
Albuquerque, NM 87107
(800) 594-9637
www.flyrodcrafters.com

Reel Life
1100 San Mateo Suite #60
Albuquerque, NM 87110
(505) 268-1693

High Desert Angler
435 S. Guadalupe
Santa Fe, NM 87501
(505) 98TROUT

Utah Fly Shops

Western Rivers Flyfisher
1071 E. 900 S.
S.L.C.,UT 84105
(800) 545-4312
www.wrflyfisher.com

High Country Flyfishers
295 S. Redwood Rd.
N. Salt Lake, UT 84054
www.hcff.com

Spinner Fall Fly Shop
2645 E. Parleys Way
S.L.C., UT 84109
(800) 959-3474
www.spinnerfall.com

Jans Mountain Outfitters
1600 Park Ave.
Park City, UT 84060
(800) 745-1020
www.jans.com

Park City Fly Shop
805 Parkview Dr.
Park City, UT 84060
(453) 645-8382
www.pcflyshop.com

Boulder Mt. Flyfishing
PO Box 1403
Boulder, UT 84716
(435) 335-7306
www.go-utah.com/flyfishing

Red Rocks Fly Shop
2 West St. George Blvd.
St. George, UT 84770
(435) 656-4665
www.redrockflyshop.com

Lee's Ferry Accommodations

Marble Canyon Lodge
(800) 726-1789
Rooms, restaurant, fly shop, store, gas and other services.

Lees Ferry Lodge
(520) 355-2231
Rooms and cafe.

Cliff Dwellers Lodge
(520) 355-2228
Rooms, food, and fly shop.

Government Resources

Arizona Tourist Bureau
Phoenix, AZ
(619) 578-7820
www.arizonatourism.com

Arizona Game & Fish Department
2221 Greenway Road
Phoenix, AZ 85023
(602) 942-3000
(800) 367-8938
www.gf.state.az.us

Bureau of Land Management
3707 N. 7th Street
PO Box 16563
Phoenix, AZ 85011
(602) 417-9200

National Parks Service
www.nps.gov
Campsite Reservations
(Selected Parks)
http://reservations.nps.gov

US Forest Service
Southwestern Region
517 Gold Ave., S.W.
Albuquerque, NM 87102
www.fs.fed.us

US Forest Service
Kaibab National Forest
800 S. 6th Street
Williams, AZ 86046
(520) 635-8200
www.fs.fed.us

US Forest Service
Cabin Reservations
www.reserveusa.com

US Fish & Wildlife
2321 W. Royal Palm Rd. #103
Phoenix, AZ 85021
(602) 640-2720
www.fws.gov

Natl. Weather Service
Flagstaff Weather Forecast Office
PO Box 16057
Bellemont, AZ 86015-6057
(928) 556-9191
www.wrh.noaa.gov/Flagstaff/

US Geological Survey
2255 N. Gemini Drive
Flagstaff, AZ 86001
wwwflag.wr.usgs.gov

Maps

National Forest Service
Coconino National Forest
Tonto National Forest
Apache-Sitgreaves National Forest
Kaibab National Forest

Earthshine
White Mountain Apache
Reservation Map

Fish 'n Map Co.
Lake Pleasant, Lees Ferry
Bartlett & Horseshoe Reservoirs
Roosevelt Lake, Apache, Canyon,
Saguaro Reservoirs

Wide World Of Maps
2626 W. Indian School Road
Phoenix, AZ 85017
(800) 279-7654

Recommended Reading

*No Nonsense Guide to
Fly Fishing In Arizona*
Glenn Tinnin

*No Nonsense Guide to
Fly Fishing In Utah*
Steve Schmidt

Fishing Arizona
G.J. Sagi

Arizona Rivers and Stream Guide
Arizona State Parks

Recreational Lakes of Arizona
J. Reinhardt, et. al.

*The Black River Book -
A Fishing & Camping Guide*
Earthshine

Arizona Road & Recreation Atlas
Benchmark Maps

Arizona Atlas & Gazetteer
DeLorme Mapping

Air Travel

American
www.aa.com
(800) 433-7300

America West
www.americawest.com
(800) 235-9292

Alaska
www.alaskaair.com
(800) 252-7522

Continental
www.flycontinental.com
(800) 525-0280

Delta
www.delta.com
(800) 221-1212

Northwest
www.nwa.com
(800) 225-2525

Southwest
www.southwest.com
(800) 435-9792

United
www.ual.com
(800) 241-6522

US Airways
www.usair.com
(800) 428-4322

Organizations

Federation of Fly Fishers
National Headquarters
(800) 618-0808
Call for local club.
www.fedflyfishers.org

*International Game
Fish Association*
300 Gulf Stream Way
Dania Beach, FL 33004
(954) 927-2628
www.igfa.org

Fly Fishing Clubs

TU Chapters
AZ - Carm Moehle
Council Chairman
519 East Thomas Road
Phoenix AZ 85012
carm.moehle@azbar.org

Old Pueblo 531
Danny Hooper
3865 E Edison Place
Tucson AZ 85716
www.optu.org

White Mountain 635
Richard Dreyer
PO Box 1237
Lakeside AZ 85929
rdreyer@agf.state.az.us

Zane Grey 463
Gary Walsh
1907 S Don Luis Circle
Mesa AZ 85202
GWalsh7797@aol.com

Dame Juliana Anglers
600 West Ray Road, Suite B-6
Chandler, AZ 85225
damejuliana@yahoo.com

Desert Fly Casters
PO Box 41271
Mesa, AZ, 85274
info@desertflycasters.com

International Women Fly Fishers
107 N. Main Street
Farmville, VA 23901
(888) 811-4933
www.intlwomenflyfishers.org

Fly Fishing The Internet

www.flyfishingconnection.com
www.flyshop.com
www.flyfishamerica.com
www.gofishin.com
www.fish-world.com
www.ufa.com
www.intlwomenflyfishers.org
www.tu.org
www.ool.com
www.azohwy.com
www.amrivers.org
www.waterworkswonders.org

Knots

www.earlham.edu/~peters/
knotlink.html
www.ozemail.com.au/~fnq/fishing

Common Fly Fishing Terms

Dun
The stage of a mayfly's development just after it has emerged and has the ability to fly.

Emerger
Stage in the development of a waterborne insect when it leaves its shuck and emerges into a flying insect.

Hatch
The time when a species of waterborne insect is emerging and becoming a flying insect.

Lake Trout
Not real trout, a member of the Char family. They not only live in lakes, they also spawn there.

Leader
A thin, clear monofilament tapered line attached to the fly line, to which either the tippet or fly is attached.

Mayfly
(Order Ephemeroptera) A very common waterborne insect with wings held in a nearly vertical position

Midge
(Order Diptera) A very small, mosquito-type fly often imitated by fly tiers.

Nymph
An undeveloped insect. Nymphs live underwater prior to emerging into a winged insect.

Rainbow Trout
(Oncorhynchus mykiss) A trout, indigenous to western and Pacific drainages. Known for the rich pinkish colorations along the fish's centerline.

Rise
A fish coming to the surface to feed.

Spinner
The final stage, after mating, when an insect falls, fatigued, to the water and dies.

Spinner Fall
When many thousands of insects, like Mayflies, fall to the water in their last mortal stage.

Spring Creek
A stream that originates from water coming up from the ground, as opposed to a freestone stream which originates from run-off or snow melt.

Stocker
A fish born and raised in a hatchery and then placed in a stream, river or lake for sport fishing.

Streamer
A fly that imitates a small fish, worm, leech, etc.

Strike Indicator
A float, most commonly foam or yarn, attached to the leader above a nymph or other wet fly.

Structure
Large objects in a stream or lake, such as big rocks, trees, dock pilings, etc., around which fish stay.

Tail Out
A location in a stream at the end of a pool, where it again becomes shallow, fast-moving water over a rocky or sandy bottom.

Terrestrial
A fly that imitates an insect born on land, e.g. grasshopper, cricket, ant, or beetle.

Tippet
Very thin, monofilament material added to the end of a leader to extend the length or to rebuild the leader after tippet has been broken off or used up tying knots.

Wet Fly
A fly fished below or in the surface film of water.

Wild
Fish born in the waters in which they are found, not raised in a hatchery.

Definitions adapted from The Easy Field Guide to Fly-Fishing Terms & Tips by our pal David Phares. For the complete list of terms, tips and some humor send $2.00 to: Primer Publishers 5738 North Central Avenue Phoenix, Arizona 85012

Other No Nonsense Titles

Business Traveler's Guide To Fly Fishing The Western States

Seasoned road warrior Bob Zeller reveals where one can fly fish within a two hour drive from every major airport in thirteen western states.

ISBN #1-892469-01-4

Traveling on business (or for some other reason)? Turn drudgery into a fun fly fishing outing. Here's how to pack, what to tell the boss and what to expect. Lots of detailed, two color maps show where to go and how to get there.

With to-the-point facts and humor Bob's 30 years of fly fishing-while-on-the-road are your guide to exploring the outdoors, not just a hotel lobby or airport lounge.

Taylor Streit's No Nonsense Guide To Fly Fishing In New Mexico

The San Juan, Cimarron, Gila, Chama, Rio Grande, mountain lakes and more.

ISBN #0-9637256-6-1

The first all inclusive guide to the top fly fishing waters in the Land of Enchantment. Since 1970 Mr. Streit has been THE New Mexico fly fishing authority and #1 professional guide. He developed many fly patterns used throughout the region, owned the Taos Fly Shop for ten years and managed a bone fishing lodge in the Bahamas. He makes winter fly fishing pilgrimages to Argentina where he escorts fly fishers and explores.

A Woman's No Nonsense Guide To Fly Fishing Favorite Waters

A First In Fly Fishing Guidebooks!

ISBN #1-892469-03-0

Forty-five of the top women fly fishing experts describe their favorite waters. From scenic spring creeks in the East, big trout waters in the Rockies to exciting Baja, Florida and Northeast saltwater: all described from the distinctive female perspective. A major donation from each printing goes to Casting For Recovery, a non-profit organization that assists women recovering from breast cancer.

Gary Graham's No Nonsense Guide To Fly Fishing Southern Baja

With this book you can fly to Baja, rent a car and go out on your own to find exciting saltwater fly fishing!

ISBN #1-892469-00-6

Mexico's Baja Peninsula is now one of the premier destinations for saltwater fly anglers. Here's the latest and best information from Baja fly fishing authority, Gary Graham. This Orvis endorsed guide has over 20 years of Baja fishing experience. He operates Baja on the Fly, a top guiding operation located in Baja's famed "East Cape" region.

Bill Mason's No Nonsense Guide To Fly Fishing In Idaho

The Henry's Fork, Salmon, Snake and Silver Creek plus 24 other waters.

ISBN #0-9637256-1-0

Mr. Mason penned the first fly fishing guidebook to Idaho in 1994. It was updated in 1996 and showcases Bill's 30 plus years of Idaho fly fishing experience.

Bill helped build a major outfitting operation at the Henry's Fork and helped open the first fly shop in Boise. In Sun Valley he developed the first fly fishing school and guiding program at Snug Fly Fishing. Bill eventually purchased the shop, renaming it Bill Mason Sun Valley Outfitters.

Harry Teel's No Nonsense Guide To Fly Fishing In Central and Southeastern Oregon

New. Updated & Reprinted. The Metolius, Deschutes, McKenzie, Owyhee, John Day and 35 other waters.

ISBN #1-892469-9-6

Mr. Teel combined his 60 years of fly fishing into the first No Nonsense fly fishing guide. It was published in 1993 and updated, expanded and improved in 1998 by Jeff Perin. Jeff owns and operates the Fly Fisher's Place, the premier fly shop in Sisters, Oregon originally owned and operated by Mr. Teel.

Jackson Streit's
No Nonsense Guide
To Fly Fishing
In Colorado

The Colorado, Rio Grande, Platte, Gunnison, mountain lakes and more.

ISBN #0-9637256-4-5

Mr. Streit fly fished Colorado for over 28 years and condensed this experience into a guidebook, published in 1995 and updated, improved and reprinted in 1997 and in 2003.

Jackson started the first guide service in the Breckenridge area and in 1985 he opened the region's first fly shop, The Mountain Angler, which he owns and manages.

Fly Fishing
California
Ken Hanley

New, Spring 2003

ISBN #1-892469-10-3

A No Nonsense overview of the best and little-known fly fishing waters in the Golden State.

Mr. Hanley and some very talented contributors like Jeff Solis, Dave Stanley, Katie Howe and others, have fly fished nearly every top water in California.

Saltwater, bass, stealhead, high mountains, they provide all you need to discover the best places to fly fish in the most geographically varied state in the U.S.

Steve Schmidt's
No Nonsense Guide
To Fly Fishing Utah

Every fly angler has heard of the famed Green River, but the rest of Utah yields extraordinary, uncrowded and little known fishing.

ISBN #0-9637256-8-8

Steve Schmidt, outfitter and owner of Western Rivers Fly Shop in Salt Lake City has explored these waters for over 27 years. He explains where to go and how to fish some of the most unique and diverse waters in the west: there's something for everybody, fly fishing mountain streams and lakes, tailwaters, bass waters and reservoirs.

Glenn Tinnin's
No Nonsense Guide
To Fly Fishing Arizona

If you are visiting the many scenic wonders of the Grand Canyon State, or moving there, bring your fly rod and this guidebook!

ISBN 1892469-02-2

Arizona has famous and little known fishing. Waters flow through desert, forest, lava fields, red rocks and canyons. Glenn Tinnin, outfitter and guide, has explored these waters for over 20 years. He explains where to go and how to fish 32 fly fishing waters including mountain streams and lakes, bass waters, reservoirs and saltwater fly fishing at Rocky Point, Mexico, a favorite and nearby getaway for Phoenix-Area anglers.

Terry Barron's
No Nonsense Guide
To Fly Fishing
Pyramid Lake

The Gem of the Desert is full of huge Lahontan Cutthroat trout.

ISBN #0-9637256-3-7

Mr. Barron is the Reno-area and Pyramid Lake fly fishing guru. He helped establish the Truckee River Fly Fishers Club and ties and works for the Reno Fly Shop.

Terry has recorded the pertinent information to fly fish the most outstanding trophy cutthroat fishery in the U.S. Where else can you get tired of catching 18-25" trout?

Gary Graham's
No NonsenseGuide
To Fly Fishing
Magdalena Bay

Word of a giant fishing paradise on Southern Baja's Pacific side has been seeping out for years. Now guide and excursion leader Gary Graham (Baja On The Fly) lays out the truth — and is it ever fascinating.

ISBN 1-892469-08-1

Mag Bay has fly fishing for highly prized Snook in mangroves, off shore marlin, calving whales from Alaska, beautiful birds, kayaking, even surfing. Fish and explore native Baja before inevitable tourism and resorts. With photos, illustrations, maps, and travel and fishing information, this is "the Bible" for this unique region.

Dave Stanley's
No Nonsense Guide
To Fly Fishing In Nevada

The Truckee, Walker, Carson, Eagle, Davis, Ruby, mountain lakes and more.

ISBN #0-9637256-2-9

Mr. Stanley is recognized nationwide as the most knowledgeable fly fisher and outdoorsman in the state of Nevada. He also travels throughout the west and other warm climes where he leads fly fishing excursions. He owns and operates the Reno Fly Shop and Truckee River Outfitters in Truckee, California.

The guide's talented coauthor, Jeff Cavender, is a Nevada native. Jeff taught fly casting and tying. He's taught and guided all over Nevada and California during the past 30 + years.

Seasons of the Metolius
The Life of a River Seen
Through the Eyes of a Fly
Fisherman
John Judy

A nature book, written by a man who makes his living fly fishing.

ISBN #1-892469-11-1

This new book describes how a beautiful riparian environment both changes and stays the same over the years. This look at nature comes from a man who makes his living working in nature and chronicles John Judy's 30 years of study, writing and fly fishing his beloved home water, the crystal clear Metolius River in central Oregon.

John Judy has been a fly fishing guide for 20 yeas and is the author of *Slack Line Strategies for Fly Fishing* (Stackpole Books). He writes the Fly Lines column for the Nugget newspaper in Sisters, Oregon and articles for other publications.

Weigh Your Catch With A Tape Measure

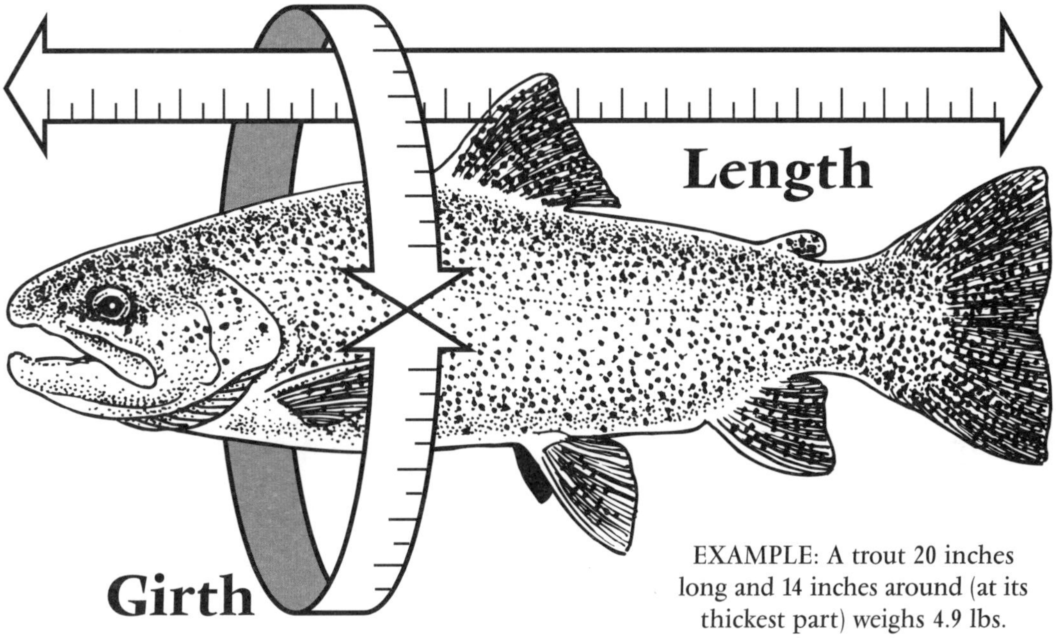

Length

Girth

EXAMPLE: A trout 20 inches long and 14 inches around (at its thickest part) weighs 4.9 lbs.

Length (inches)
Tip of nose to notch at the center of tail.

	0	10	12	14	16	18	20	22	24	26	28	30
8		.8	1.0	1.1	1.3	1.4	1.6	1.8	1.9	2.1	2.2	2.4
10		1.3	1.5	1.8	2.0	2.3	2.5	2.8	3.0	3.3	3.5	3.8
12		1.8	2.2	2.5	2.9	3.2	3.6	4.0	4.3	4.7	5.0	5.4
14		2.5	2.9	3.4	3.9	4.4	4.9	5.4	5.9	6.4	6.9	7.4
16		3.2	3.8	4.5	5.1	5.8	6.4	7.0	7.7	8.3	9.0	9.6
18		4.1	4.9	5.7	6.5	7.3	8.1	8.9	9.7	10.5	11.3	12.2
20		5.0	6.0	7.0	8.0	9.0	10.0	11.0	12.0	13.0	14.0	15.0

Girth (inches)

Courtesy of Ralph & Lisa Cutter's California School of Flyfishing • P.O. Box 8212 • Truckee, CA 96162 • 1-800-58-TROUT

Fly Fishing Knots

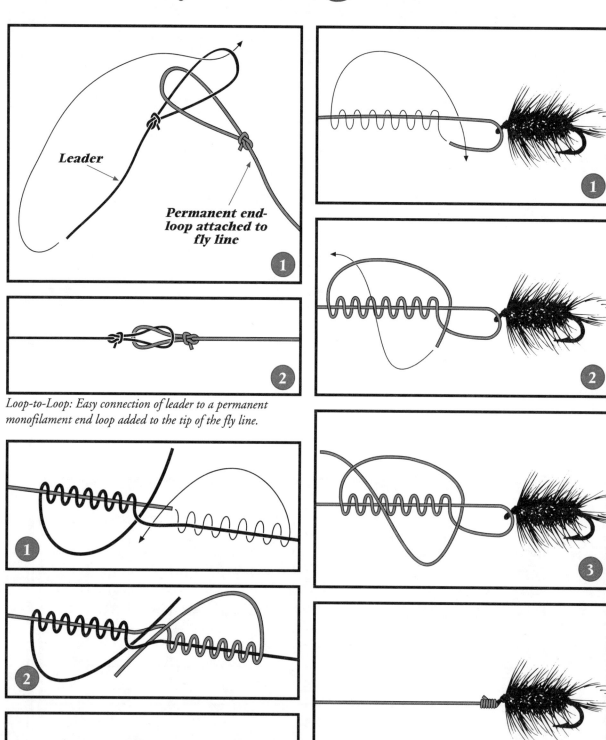

Leader

Permanent end-loop attached to fly line

Loop-to-Loop: Easy connection of leader to a permanent monofilament end loop added to the tip of the fly line.

Blood Knot: Use this knot to connect sections of leader tippet material. Hard to tie, but worth the effort.

Improved Clinch Knot: Use this knot to attach the fly to the end of the tippet. Remember to moisten the knot before pulling it up tight.

Fly Fishing Knots

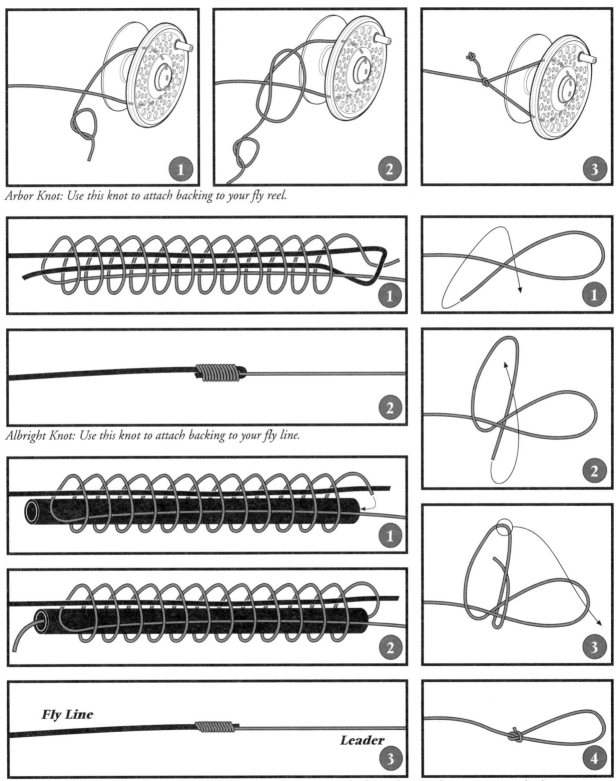

Arbor Knot: Use this knot to attach backing to your fly reel.

Albright Knot: Use this knot to attach backing to your fly line.

Fly Line

Leader

Nail Knot: Use a nail, needle or a tube to tie this knot, which connects the forward end of the fly line to the butt end of the leader. Follow this with a Perfection Loop. and you've got a permanent end loop that allows easy leader changes.

Perfection Loop: Use this knot to create a loop in the butt end of the leader.

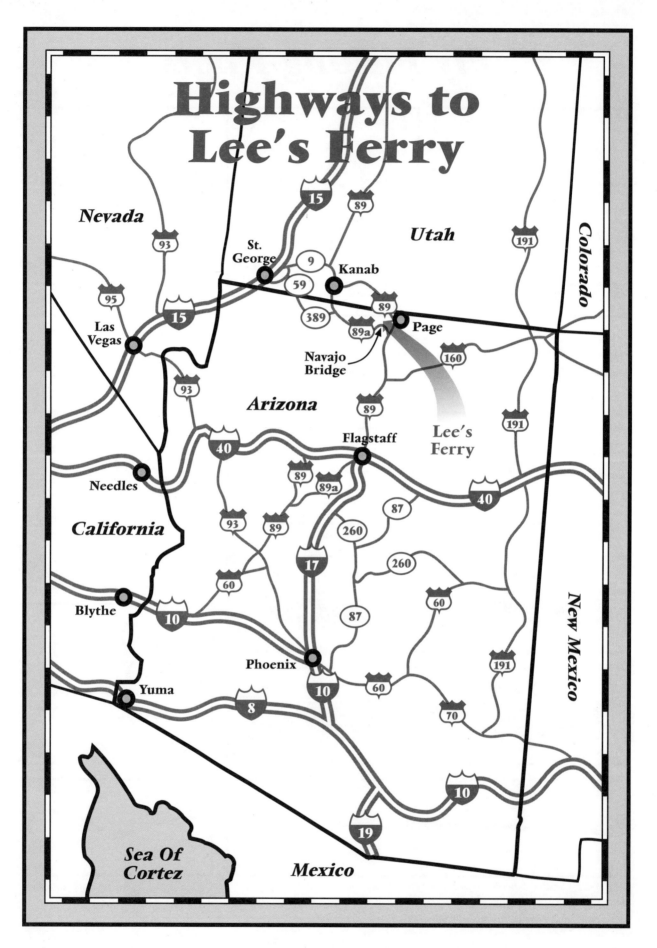

Highways to Lee's Ferry

Nevada

Utah

Colorado

93

St. George

Kanab

15

89

191

9

59

389

89

95

89a

Page

Las Vegas

Navajo Bridge

160

93

Arizona

89

191

Lee's Ferry

40

Flagstaff

Needles

89

89a

40

California

93

89

87

260

260

17

60

60

New Mexico

87

Blythe

10

Phoenix

191

Yuma

10

60

8

70

10

19

Sea Of Cortez

Mexico

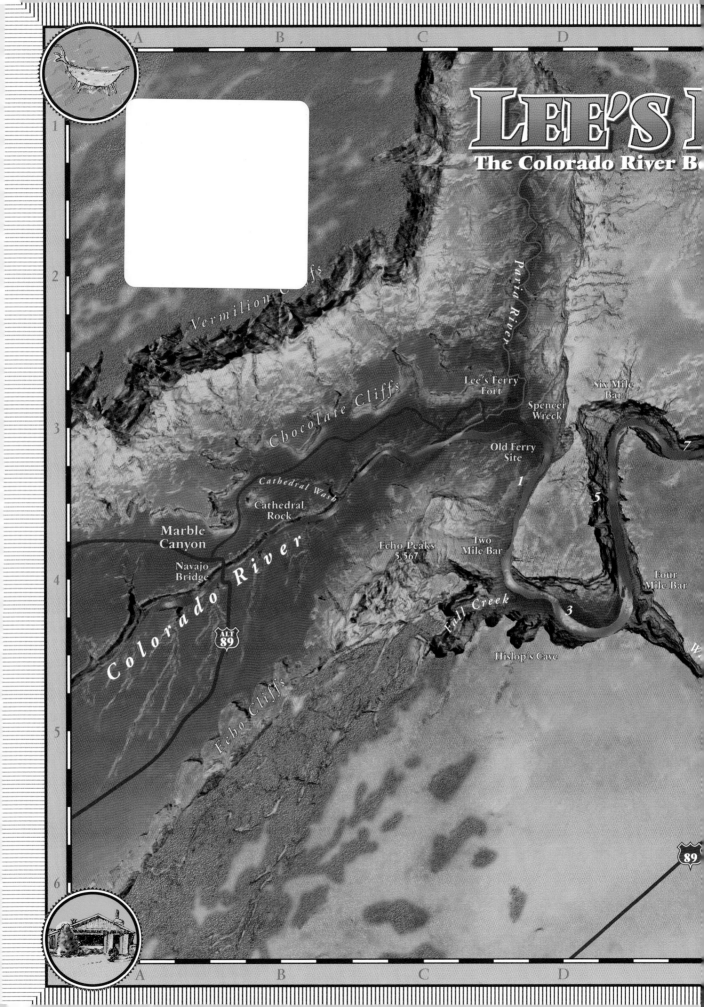

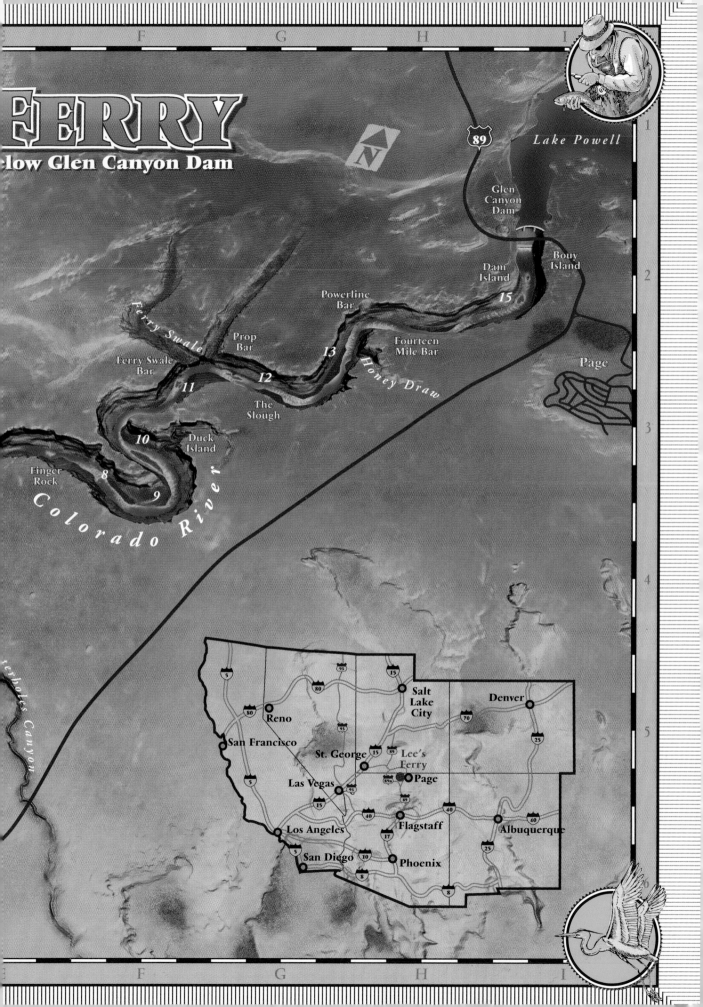

FERRY
Below Glen Canyon Dam

89 Lake Powell

N

Glen Canyon Dam

Dam Island

Bouy Island

15

Powerline Bar

Ferry Swale

Prop Bar

Fourteen Mile Bar

13

Honey Draw

Page

Ferry Swale Bar

12

11

The Slough

10

Duck Island

Finger Rock

8

9

Colorado River

Waterholes Canyon

5

93

15

Salt Lake City

Denver

80

80

Reno

80

93

70

25

San Francisco

St. George

15

89

Lee's Ferry

5

Las Vegas

89

Page

15

91

89

40

40

Los Angeles

40

Flagstaff

Albuquerque

5

17

25

San Diego

10

Phoenix

8

8